The Blood Knot

A PLAY IN THREE ACTS

By Athol Fugard

D0284152

SAMUEL FRENCH, INC.

45 West 25th Street   NEW YORK 10010

7623 Sunset Boulevard   HOLLYWOOD 90046

LONDON   *TORONTO*

STORY OF THE PLAY

THE BLOOD KNOT is a parable of two brothers—one white-skinned, one black—sharing a hovel on the outskirts of Port Elizabeth, committed to a shifting, abrasive relationship, which reflects all the larger fears and anguish of racial issues. On the stage, Athol Fugard's play is poignant and compelling; on the printed page, it stands the test of readability, blessed as it is by sensitive and imaginitive dialogue. THE BLOOD KNOT was first produced in South Africa in 1961, with the author in the role of Morris and Zakes Mokae as Zachariah. It was a theatrical milestone in that country—both for its dramatic technique and for its outspoken theme. One reviewer spoke of "its subtlety, its unexpected richness, its sparks of penetrating dialogue, its humour and its deep pain." Several reviewers wisely predicted that Mr. Fugard's play would find audiences throughout the world. Subsequently it was produced successfully in London, and in March, 1964, the celebrated American production opened at the Cricket Theatre in New York, with J.D. Cannon and James Earl Jones as the brothers.

INTRODUCTION

You and me. That is how it starts. The two factors in an equation which resolves out into either heaven or hell, and most likely both. If there is a human predicament, this is it. There is another existence and it feels, and I feel it feels, yet I am impotent. I cannot take over. I want to. But I cannot. There is nothing I can do except stand by and watch.

At the end of the first scene of THE BLOOD KNOT there is a moment — it was cut in the American production — when Morris puts on Zachariah's coat. Zachariah is sleeping and Morris sits alone on stage. "You get right inside a man when you can wrap up in the smell of him. . . ," Morris says. ". . . your flesh, you see, has an effect on me. The sight of it, the feel of it . . . it . . . it feels, you see. Pain, and all those dumb dreams . . ." And just before the curtain comes down on that scene: "I saw you again after all those years . . . and it hurt."

Then — responsibility. *You* are the "other man," the other existence over which I have no control ultimately, yet somehow I feel that I've got something to do with it. I don't feel innocent. So then how guilty am I? In any case, what did I do? I mean, even in my own life none of the final facts was ever given me as a choice. There I was one day, here I am now, tomorrow . . . who knows? Maybe guilt isn't all *doing*. Maybe just *being* is some sort of sin. I'm sure Morris says that somewhere. If he hasn't, he should.

So what do we do? Let's work it out, Morris says. Talking helps, man. You mean you didn't know that? You find the answers to things, the way we are going to find the answer to this problem. How about me wrapping you up? You see, if only you will stop feeling things . . . certain things . . . the ones that hurt . . . it will be a lot easier. 'S true's God, Zachie. Cross my heart and hope to die. It will help . . . me.

But there are two sides to every sad story. In the first scene — the brothers have been living together again for about a year — Zachariah turns to Morrie and says: "I was doing all right . . . wasn't I? Minnie used to come. He had a bottle, or I had a bottle, but we both had a good time. And then you came . . ." "Say it," Morris urges. Zachariah finishes his statement. " . . . then you came. That's all. . . . A knocking on my door on a Friday night . . . and it was you standing there . . ."

If Morrie is something gone sour, gone sick, then Zachariah is the contact, the man who picked it up. Nothing is as honest as doing and this was Zachariah's level before that Friday night. But nothing is as contagious as thinking and that is what Morris brought back into the shack. In the third scene Zachariah says: "I'm a man with a taste for thoughts these days." Something's happened.

Finally there are the specifics. I am a South African, white-skinned. There are three million of us. There are also twelve million dark-skinned South Africans. At the very end of the play, after a game which had the brothers looking into the maws of hell, and which they will surely play again tomorrow night, and the night after that — after this game and just before sleep the dark-skinned brother asks: "What is it, Morrie? The two of us . . . you know . . . in here?" The light-skinned brother replies, "Home." The other then asks: "Is there no other way?" Morris's reply is on the last page of this book.

Athol Fugard

CHARACTERS

There are two characters, ZACHARIAH and MORRIS. ZACHARIAH is dark-skinned and MORRIS is light-skinned.

SETTING

All the action takes place in a one-room shack in the Non-White location of Korsten, near Port Elizabeth, South Africa. The walls are a patchwork of scraps of corrugated iron, packing-case wood, flattened cardboard boxes and old hessian bags. There is one door, one window (no curtains), two beds, a table and two chairs. Also in evidence is a cupboard of sorts with an oil stove, a kettle and a few pots. The shack is tidy and swept, but this only emhances the poverty of its furnishings. Over one of the beds is a shelf on which are a few books and an alarm clock.

The Blood Knot

ACT ONE

Late afternoon. Lying on his bed, the one with the shelf, and staring up at the ceiling, is MORRIS. After a few seconds he stands up on the bed, looks at the alarm clock and then lies down again in the same position. Time passes. The alarm rings and MORRIS jumps purposefully to his feet. He knows exactly what he is going to do. First, he winds and resets the clock, then lights the oilstove and puts on a kettle of water. Next, he places an enamel washbasin on the floor in front of the other bed and lays out a towel. He feels the kettle on the stove and then goes to the door and looks out. Nothing. He wanders aimlessly around the room for a few more seconds, pausing at the window for a long look at whatever lies beyond. Eventually he is back at the door again and, after a short wait, he sees someone coming. A second burst of activity. He places a packet of footsalts beside the basin and finally replaces the kettle. ZACHARIAH comes in through the door. Their meeting is without words. MORRIS nods and ZACHARIAH grunts on his way to the bed, where he sits down, drags off his shoes and rolls up his trousers. While he does this, MORRIS sprinkles footsalts into the basin and then sits back on his haunches and waits. ZACHARIAH dips his feet into the basin, sighs with satisfaction, but stops abruptly when he sees MORRIS smile. He frowns, pretends to think and makes a great business of testing the water with his foot.

7

ZACHARIAH. Not as hot as last night, hey?

MORRIS. Last night you said it was too hot.

ZACHARIAH. (*thinks about this*) That's what I mean.

MORRIS. So what is it? Too hot or too cold?

ZACHARIAH. When?

MORRIS. Now.

ZACHARIAH. Luke-ish. (*bends forward and smells*) New stuff?

MORRIS. Yes.

ZACHARIAH. Oh! Let's see. (*MORRIS hands him the packet. ZACHARIAH first smells it, then takes out a pinch between thumb and forefinger.*) It's also white.

MORRIS. Yes, but it is different stuff.

ZACHARIAH. The other lot was also white but it didn't help, hey?

MORRIS. This is definitely different stuff, Zach. (*pointing*) See. There's the name. Radium Salts. (*ZACHARIAH is not convinced. MORRIS fetches a second packet.*) Here's the other. Schultz's Foot Salts.

ZACHARIAH. (*taking the second packet and looking inside*) They look the same, don't they? (*smells*) But they smell different. You know something? I think the old lot smells nicest. What do you say we go back to the old lot?

MORRIS. But you just said it didn't help!

ZACHARIAH. But it smells better.

MORRIS. It's not the smell, Zach. You don't go by the smell, man.

ZACHARIAH. No?

MORRIS. It's the healing properties.

ZACHARIAH. Maybe.

MORRIS. (*taking back the new packet*) Listen to this . . . (*reads*) "For all agonies of the joints: Lumbago, rheumatism, tennis elbows, housemaid's knees;

also ideal for bunions, corns, calluses" — that's what you got. (*ZACHARIAH let's him finish, examining the old packet while MORRIS reads.*)

ZACHARIAH. How much that new stuff cost?

MORRIS. Why?

ZACHARIAH. Tell me, man!

MORRIS. (*aware of what is coming*) Listen, Zach. It's the healing properties. Price has nothing . . .

ZACHARIAH. (*insistent*) How — much — does — that — cost?

MORRIS. Two and six.

ZACHARIAH. (*with a small laugh*) You know something?

MORRIS. Yes, yes, I know what you're going to say.

ZACHARIAH. This old stuff, which isn't so good, is three a bob. A six-pence more! (*He starts to laugh.*)

MORRIS. So? Listen, Zach. No. Wait man! Price, Zach . . . ZACH! Do you want to listen or don't you? (*ZACHARIAH is laughing loud in triumph.*) PRICE HAS GOT NOTHING TO DO WITH IT!

ZACHARIAH. Then why is this more money?

MORRIS. Profit. He's making more profit on the old stuff. Satisfied?

ZACHARIAH. So?

MORRIS. So.

ZACHARIAH. Oh. (*slowly*) So he's making more profit on the old stuff. (*The thought comes.*) But that's what you been buying, man! Ja — and with my money, remember! So it happens to be my profit he's making. Isn't that so? I work for the money. Not him. (*He is getting excited and now stands in the basin of water.*) Ja. I see it now. I do the bloody work — all day long — in the sun. Not him. It's my stinking feet that got the hardnesses. But he goes and makes my profit. (*steps out of the basin*) I want to work this out, please. How long you been buying that old stuff? Four weeks? That makes four packets, hey? So you say sixpence profit . . . which comes to . . . two bob . . . isn't that so? Whose? Mine. Who's got it? Him . . . him . . . some dirty, rotting, stinking, creeping, little . . .

MORRIS. But we are buying the cheap salts now Zach! (*pause*) He's not going to get the profits anymore. And what is more still, the new salts is better. (*The thread of ZACHARIAH's reasoning has been broken. He stares blankly at Morris.*)

ZACHARIAH. I still say the old smells sweeter.

MORRIS. I tell you what. I'll give you a double dose. One of the old and one of the new . . . together! That way you get the healing properties and the smell. By God, that sounds like a cure! How's that, Zach? Okay?

ZACHARIAH. Okay. (*He goes to the bed, sits down and once again soaks his feet.*) You got any more warm? (*MORRIS pours the last of the hot water into the basin. ZACHARIAH now settles down to enjoy the luxury of his footbath. MORRIS helps him off with his tie, and afterwards puts away his shoes.*)

MORRIS. How did it go today?

ZACHARIAH. He's got me standing again.

MORRIS. At the gate?

ZACHARIAH. Ja.

MORRIS. But didn't you tell him, Zach? I told you to tell him that your feet are calloused and that you wanted to go back to the pots.

ZACHARIAH. I did.

MORRIS. And then?

ZACHARIAH. He said: Go to the gate or go to hell.

MORRIS. That's and insult.

ZACHARIAH. What's the other one?

MORRIS. Injury!

ZACHARIAH. No. The long one, man.

MORRIS. Inhumanity!

ZACHARIAH. Ja. That's what I think it is. My inhumanity *from him.* "Go to the gate or go to hell." What do they think I am?

MORRIS. What about me?

ZACHARIAH. (*anger*) Okay. What do you think I am?

MORRIS. No, Zach! Good heavens! You got it all wrong. What do *they* think *I* am, when they think what *you* are. Yes. I'm on your side, they're on theirs. I couldn't be living here and not be on yours, could I? (*MORRIS is helping ZACHARIAH off with his coat. When ZACHARIAH is not looking he smells it.*) Zach, I think we must borrow Minnie's bath again.

ZACHARIAH. Okay.

MORRIS. What about me? Do I smell?

ZACHARIAH. No. (*pause*) Have I started again? (*MORRIS doesn't answer. ZACHARIAH laughs.*) What's that thing you say, Morrie? The one about smelling?

MORRIS. (*quoting*) "The rude odours of manhood."

ZACHARIAH. "The rude odours of manhood." And the other one? The long one?

MORRIS. No smell? (*ZACHARIAH nods.*)
"No smell doth stink as sweet as labour.
'This joyous times when man and man
Do work and sweat in common toil,
When all the world's my neighbour."

ZACHARIAH. "When all the world's my neighbour." (*ZACHARIAH starts drying his feet with the towel. MORRIS empties the basin and puts it away.*) Minnie.

MORRIS. What about Minnie?

ZACHARIAH. Our neighbour. Strange thing about Minnie. He doesn't come anymore.

MORRIS. I don't miss him.

ZACHARIAH. You don't remember. I'm talking about before you.

MORRIS. Of course I remember. Didn't he come that once when I was here? And sit all night and say nothing?

ZACHARIAH. Before that, Morrie. I'm meaning before your time, man. He came every night. Ja! Me and him used to go out — together, you know — quite a bit. (*pause*) How did I forget a thing like that!

MORRIS. What are you talking about?

ZACHARIAH. Me and Minnie going out! Almost every night . . . and I've forgotten. (*pause*) How long you been here?

MORRIS. About a year.

ZACHARIAH. Only one miserable year and I have forgotten just like that! Just like it might not hardly have never happened!

MORRIS. The year has flown by.

ZACHARIAH. You never wabt to go out, Morrie.

MORRIS. So I don't want to go out. Ask me why and I'll tell you. Come on.

ZACHARIAH. Why?

MORRIS. Because we got plans, remember? We're saving for a future, which is something Minnie didn't have.

ZACHARIAH. Ja. He doesn't come no more.

MORRIS. You said that already, you know. I heard you the first time.

ZACHARIAH. I was just thinking. I remembered him today. I was at the gate. It was lunchtime. I was eating my bread.

MORRIS. Did you like the peanut butter?

ZACHARIAH. And then it comes, the thought: What the hell has happened to old Minnie?

MORRIS. Zach, I was asking you —

ZACHARIAH. Wait, man! I'm remembering it now. He used to come, with a guitar to this room, to me, to his

friend, old Zachariah, waiting for him here. Friday
nights it was, when a ou's got pay in his pocket and
there's no work tomorrow and Minnie is coming. There
was a friend for a man! He could laugh, could Minnie,
and drink! He knew the spots, I'm telling you . . . and
what else? Ja! (*reverently*) Minnie had music! Listen,
he could do a *vastrap,* that man, non-stop, on all strings,
at once. He knew the lot. Polka, tickey-draai, opskud
en uitkap, ek sê . . . that was jollification for you, with
Minnie. So, when I'm waiting here, and I hear that
guitar in the street, at my door, I'm happy! "It's you," I
shout. "I know it's you." He pretends he isn't there, you
see. "Minnie," I call. "Minnie!" So what does he do
then? He gives me a quick chik-a-doem in G. He knows
I like G. "It's Friday night, Minnie." "Doem-doem," he
says. And then I'm laughing. "You bugger! You
motherless bastard." So I open the door. And what's
that he got in his hand? Golden Moments at two bob a
bottle. Standing just right on that spot out there in the
street with his bottle and his music and laughing with
me. "Zach," he says, "Ou Pellie, tonight is the night—"
(*The alarm goes off.*) . . . is the night . . .
(*ZACHARIAH loses the thread of his story. By the
time the alarm stops, he has forgotten what he was saying. The moment the alarm goes off MORRIS springs to
his feet and busies himself at the table with their supper.
ZACHARIAH eventually goes back to the bed.*)

MORRIS. I got polony and chips tonight. Variety spiced
with life, as they say. (*MORRIS watches ZACH-
ARIAH surreptitiously from the table.*) I been thinking,
Zach. It's time we started making some definite plans. I
mean . . . we've agreed on the main idea. The thing now
is to find the right place. (*pause*) Zach? (*pause*) We
have agreed, haven't we?

ZACHARIAH. About what?

MORRIS. Hell, man. The future. It is going to be a small two-man farm, just big enough for you and me; or what is it going to be?

ZACHARIAH. Ja.

MORRIS. Right. We agree. Now, I'm saying we got to find the right place. (*pause*) Zach! What's the matter with you?

ZACHARIAH. I was trying to remember what I was saying about Minnie. There was something else.

MORRIS. Now listen, Zach! You said yourself he doesn't come no more. So what are you doing thinking about it? Here am I putting our future to you and you don't even listen. The farm, Zach! Remember, man? Picture it! Picking our own fruit. Chasing those damned baboons helter-skelter in the koppies. Chopping the firewood trees . . . and a cow . . . and a horse . . . and little chickens. Isn't it exciting? Well, I haven't been sitting still, Zachie. The right place. It's a big world this. A big, bloody world. Korsten, my friend, is just the beginning. (*MORRIS fetches an old map from the shelf over his bed.*) Now, I want you to take a look at this. You want to know what it is? A map . . . of Africa. Now, this is the point, Zach. There . . . and there . . . and there . . . and down here . . . Do you see it? Blank. Large, blank spaces. Not a town, not a road, not even those thin little red lines. And, notice, they're green. That means grass. I reckon we should be able to get a few acres in one of these blank spaces for next to nothing. (*ZACHARIAH, bored, goes to the window and looks out.*) You listening, Zach?

ZACHARIAH. Ja.

MORRIS. This is not just talk, you know. It's serious. I'm not smiling. You say I don't want to get out? My reply is that I do, but I want to get right out. You think I like it here more than you? You should have been here this afternoon. The wind was blowing again. Coming this way it was, right across the lake. You should have smelt it. I'm telling you that water has gone bad. Really rotten! And what about the factories there on the other side? Hey? And the lavatories all around us? They've left no room for a man to breathe. But when we go, Zach, together, and we got a place to go, our farm in the future . . . that will be different. (*ZACHARIAH has been at the window all the time, staring out. He now sees something which makes him laugh. Just a chuckle to begin with, but with a suggestion of lechery.*) What's so funny?

ZACHARIAH. Come here.

MORRIS. What's there?

ZACHARIAH. Two donkeys, man. You know. (*MORRIS makes no move to the window. ZACHARIAH stays there, laughing from time to time.*)

MORRIS. Yes. It's not just talk. When you bring your pay home tomorrow and we put away the usual, guess what we will have? Forty-five pounds. If it wasn't for me you wouldn't have nothing. Ever think about that? You talk about going out, but forty-five pounds—

ZACHARIAH. (*breaking off in the middle of a laugh*) Hey! I remember now! By hell! About Minnie. (*His voice expresses vast disbelief.*) How did I forget? Where has it gone? It was . . . ja . . . ja . . . It was a woman! That's what we had when we went out at night. Woman! (*MORRIS doesn't move. He stares at ZACHARIAH blankly. When the latter pauses for a second MORRIS speaks again in an almost normal voice.*)

MORRIS. Supper is ready. (*ZACHARIAH loses the train of his thought, as with the alarm clock, earlier. MORRIS sits down.*) So . . . where were we? Yes. Our plans. When, Zach? That's another thing we got to think about. Should we take our chance with a hundred pounds, one hundred and fifty? I mean . . . we can even wait till there is three hundred, isn't that so? (*ZACHARIAH is still standing.*) Bring that chair over there, man, and sit down and eat. (*MORRIS has already started on his supper. As if hypnotized by the sound of the other man's voice, ZACHARIAH fetches the chair and sits.*) So what are we going to do, you ask? This. Find out what the deposit, cash, on a small two man farm, in one of those blank spaces, is. Take some bread, man. (*Offering a slice, ZACHARIAH leaves the table.*) You finished?

ZACHARIAH. Ja.

MORRIS. Left your chips, Zach. What's wrong?

ZACHARIAH. Not nice chips.

MORRIS. Same as always. Ferreira's.

ZACHARIAH. I — said — they — aren't — nice — chips!

MORRIS. And the bread, too?

ZACHARIAH. Ja. And the bread too.

MORRIS. Okay. But we always have polony and chips on a Friday. (*ZACHARIAH says nothing.*) I mean . . . that was an agreement, like fish on Thursday.

ZACHARIAH. (*in a rage*) Well, I'm telling you now! They — aren't — nice — chips! (*MORRIS looks blankly at him. This enrages ZACHARIAH even more.*) Look at them, will you! This one! Now I just want to know one thing! Does this look like it came from a potato? Hey? And this one? Now tell me. Would you even give this to a horse?

MORRIS. Why a horse?

ZACHARIAH. Why not? Some stinking horse.

MORRIS. They don't eat . . .

ZACHARIAH. You just keep quiet, Morris, and let me

finish this time, and don't think I'm going to get lost in my words again. That bloody clock of yours doesn't go off till bed-time, so I got plenty of time to talk. So just you shut up, please! Now this chip . . . and the whole, rotten, stinking lot. (*ZACHARIAH is throwing them all around the room.*) If my profit is tied up in this as well, I'll go out and murder the bastard. Well? Is it?

MORRIS. I don't think so.

ZACHARIAH. So you don't think so. How much you pay for them?

MORRIS. Sixpence. Like always.

ZACHARIAH. Like always. Well, all I can say is that he's lucky, because if I ever meet that Ferreira, I'm going to ask him what he thinks I am.

MORRIS. Come on now, Zach. I was telling you about the farm.

ZACHARIAH. Stop it! I won't listen! You're not going to make me forget. (*rushes across to the other side where his jacket is hanging, begins to put it on*) What do you think I am, hey? Two legs and trousers. I'm a man. And in this world there is also woman, and the one has got to get the other. Even donkeys know that. What I want to know now, right this very now, is why me, Zach, a man, for a whole miserable little year has had none. I was doing all right before that, wasn't I? Minnie used to come. He had a bottle, or I had a bottle, but we both had a good time, for a long time. And then you came . . . and . . . (*pause*)

MORRIS. Say it.

ZACHARIAH. . . . then you came. That's all. (*ZACHARIAH's violence is ebbing away. Perplexity takes its place.*) You knocked on the door. It was Friday night. I remember, I got a fright. A knocking on my door on Friday night? On *my* door? Who? Not Minnie.

Minnie's coming all right, but not like that. So I had a look, and it was you standing there, and you said something, hey? What did I say? "Come in." Didn't I? "Come in," I said. And when we had eaten I said, "Come out with me and a friend of mine, called Minnie." Then you said: "Zach, let us spend tonight talking." Ja, that's it. That's all. A whole year of spending tonights talking, talking. I'm sick of talking. I'm sick of this room.

MORRIS. I know, Zach. (*He speaks quietly, soothingly.*) That's why we got plans.

ZACHARIAH. But I was in here ten years without plans and never needed them!

MORRIS. Time, Zach. It passes.

ZACHARIAH. I was in here ten years and didn't worry about my feet, or a future, or having supper on time! But I had fun and Minnie's music!

MORRIS. That's life for you.

ZACHARIAH. I want woman.

MORRIS. I see. I see that, Zach. Believe me, I do. But let me think about it. Okay? Now finish your supper and I'll think about it. (*MORRIS puts his own plate of food in front of ZACHARIAH and then moves around the room picking up the food that ZACHARIAH swept to the floor.*) You get fed up with talking, I know, but it helps, doesn't it? You find the answers to things like we are going to find the answer to your problem. I mean . . . Look what it's done for us already. Our plans! Our future! You should be grateful, man. And remember what I said. You're not the only one who's sick of this room. It also gets me down. (*turning to ZACHARIAH, leaving the window*) Have you noticed, Zach, the days are getting shorter again, the nights longer? Autumn is in our smelly air. It's the time I came back, hey! About a year ago! We should have remembered what day it was, though. Would have made a good birthday, don't you think? A candle on a cake for the day that Morrie came back to Zach. Yes. That's bitter. Not to have remembered what day it was. I mean . . . so much started for both of us. I reckon it's one of the hard things in life to begin again when you're already in the middle. (*ZACHARIAH leaves the table and goes to his bed.*) You finished?

ZACHARIAH. Ja.

MORRIS. (*Pause. MORRIS makes the sandwiches.*) Has it helped, Zach?

ZACHARIAH. What?

MORRIS. The talking.

ZACHARIAH. Helped what?

MORRIS. About . . . woman.

ZACHARIAH. No. You said you was going to think about it and me.

MORRIS. Shall I talk some more?

ZACHARIAH. Let me! (*He speaks eagerly. The first sign of life since the outburst.*) Let me talk about . . . woman.

MORRIS. You think it wise?

ZACHARIAH. You said it helps. I want to help.

MORRIS. Go on.

ZACHARIAH. You know what I was remembering, Morrie? As I sat there?

MORRIS. No.

ZACHARIAH. (*soft, nostalgic smile*) The first one. My very first one. You was already gone. It was in those years. (*sigh*) Her name was Connie.

MORRIS. That's a lovely name, Zach.

ZACHARIAH. Connie . . .

MORRIS. You were happy, hey?

ZACHARIAH. Ja.

MORRIS. Don't be shy. Tell me more.

ZACHARIAH. We were young. Her mother did washing. Connie used to buy blue soap from the Chinaman on the corner.

MORRIS. Your sweetheart, hey!

ZACHARIAH. She called me a black hotnot, the bitch, so I waited for her. She had tits like fruits. So I waited for her in the bushes. She was coming along alone. Hell! Don't I remember Connie now. Coming along alone, she was, and I was waiting in the bushes. (*laughs*) She got a fright, she did. She tried to fight, to bite—

MORRIS. All right, Zach!

ZACHARIAH. She might have screamed, but when I had her—

MORRIS. That's enough! (*pause*)

ZACHARIAH. That was Connie. (*He broods.*)

MORRIS. Feeling better?

ZACHARIAH. A little.

MORRIS. Talking helps, doesn't it? I said so. You find the answers to things.

ZACHARIAH. Talking to one would help me even more.

MORRIS. Yes . . . (*pause*) You mean to a woman?

ZACHARIAH. I'm telling you, Morrie, I mean it, man. With all my heart.

MORRIS. (*The idea is coming.*) There's a thought coming, Zach.

ZACHARIAH. There is?

MORRIS. In fact I think we got it.

ZACHARIAH. What?

MORRIS. The answer to your problem, man.

ZACHARIAH. Woman?

MORRIS. That's it! You said talking to one would help

you, didn't you? So what about writing? Just as good, isn't it, if she writes back?

ZACHARIAH. Who . . . who you talking about?

MORRIS. A pen-pal, Zach! A corresponding pen-pal of the opposite sex! Don't you know them? (*ZACHARIAH's face is blank.*) It's a woman, you see! (*looking for newspaper*) She wants a man friend, but she's in another town, so she writes to him—to you!

ZACHARIAH. I don't know her.

MORRIS. You will. You're her pen-pal!

ZACHARIAH. I don't write letters.

MORRIS. I will.

ZACHARIAH. Then it's your pen-pal.

MORRIS. No, Zach. You tell me what to say. You see, she writes to you. She doesn't even know about me. Can't you see it, man? A letter to Mr. Zachariah Pietersen—you—from her.

ZACHARIAH. I don't read letters.

MORRIS. I'll read them to you.

ZACHARIAH. From a woman.

MORRIS. From a woman. You can take your pick.

ZACHARIAH. (*now really interested*) Hey!

MORRIS. There's so many.

ZACHARIAH. Is that so!

MORRIS. Big ones, small ones.

ZACHARIAH. What do you know about that!

MORRIS. Young ones, old ones.

ZACHARIAH. No. Not the old ones, Morrie. (*excited*) The young ones, on the small side.

MORRIS. (*happy*) Just take your pick.

ZACHARIAH. Okay. I will.

MORRIS. (*studying a newspaper*) There's three women here. The young ladies Ethel Lange, Nellie de Wet and Betty Jones.

ZACHARIAH. (*hopefully*) There's no Connie, is there, Morrie?

MORRIS. No. Now, before you decide, I suppose I'd better tell you about them.

ZACHARIAH. What do you know about them?

MORRIS. It's written down here, man. Listen . . . (*reads*) "Ethel Lange, 10 de Villiers Street, Oudtshoorn. I am eighteen years old and well-developed and would like to correspond with a gent of sober habits and a good outlook on life. My interests are nature, rock-and-roll, swimming and a happy future. My motto is, 'rolling stones gather no moss.' Please note: I promise to reply faithfully." How's that?

ZACHARIAH. Well-developed.

MORRIS. She gives a ou a clear picture, hey! Here's the next one. (*reads*) "Nellie de Wet" . . . she's in Bloemfontein . . . "Twenty-two and no strings attached. Would like letters from men of my age or older. My interests are beauty contests and going out. A snap with the first letter, please." (*pause*) That's all there is to her. I think I preferred Ethel.

ZACHARIAH. Ja. And what do I know how old I am?

MORRIS. Exactly, Zach! "My age or older?" Where does she think she comes from?

ZACHARIAH. Bloemfontein.

MORRIS. Yes. Last one. (*reads*) "Betty Jones. Roodepoort. Young and pleasing personality. I'd like to write to gentlemen friends of maturity. No ducktails need reply. My hobby at the moment is historical films, but I'm prepared to go back to last year's, which was autograph hunting. I would appreciate a photograph." She's got a education. Anyway . . . it's up to you. Take your pick.

ZACHARIAH. (*after thinking about it*) Hey, Morrie! Let's take all three.

MORRIS. No, Zach.

ZACHARIAH. Aw, come on.

MORRIS. You don't understand.

ZACHARIAH. Just for sports, man!

MORRIS. I don't think they'd allow that. (*pause, emphatic*) Listen, Zach, you must take this serious.

ZACHARIAH. Okay.

MORRIS. (*losing patience*) Well, it's no good saying "Okay" like that!

ZACHARIAH. Okay!

MORRIS. What's the use, Zach? You ask me to help you, and when I do, you're not interested anymore.

ZACHARIAH. I can't get hot about a name on a piece of paper. It's not real to me.

MORRIS. (*outraged*) Not real! (*reads*) "I am eighteen years old and well-developed" . . . eighteen years old and well-developed! If I called that Connie it would be real enough, wouldn't it?

ZACHARIAH. (*His face lighting up.*) Ja!

MORRIS. So the only difference is a name. This is Ethel and not Connie . . . which makes no difference to being eighteen years old and well-developed! Think, man!

ZACHARIAH. (*without hesitation*) Look, Morrie, I'll take her.

MORRIS. That's better. So it's going to be Miss Ethel Lange at 10 de Villers Street, Oudtshoorn, who would like to correspond with a gent of sober habits and a good outlook on life. (*putting down the paper*) Yes, she's the one for you all right. And I know what we do. How about asking Ethel to take a snapshot of herself? So that you can know what *her* outlook is. Then—just think of it—you can see her, hear from her, write to her, correspond with her, post your letter off to her . . . Hell, man! What more do you want! (*ZACHARIAH smiles.*) No! Don't tell me. That's something else. This is pen-pals, and you got yourself Ethel in Oudtshoorn. Now, come and we'll get started on our first letter to her. (*pause*) Eighteen years old and well-developed. You still want her? (*ZACHARIAH looks up. MORRIS moves to the table where he sorts out a piece of writing paper, a pencil and an envelope.*) I've got everything ready. One day I must show you how. Maybe have a go at a letter yourself. Address in the top righthand corner. Mr. Zachariah Pietersen, Korsten, P.O. Port Elizabeth. Okay, now we take aim and fire away. (*He waits for ZACHARIAH.*) Well?

ZACHARIAH. What?

MORRIS. Speak to Ethel.

ZACHARIAH. (*shy*) Go jump in a lake, man.

MORRIS. No, listen, Zach. I'm sitting here ready to write. You must speak up.

ZACHARIAH. What?

MORRIS. To begin with, address her.

ZACHARIAH. What!

MORRIS. Address her.

ZACHARIAH. Oudtshoorn.

MORRIS. You're not understanding. Now imagine, if there was a woman, and you want to say something to her, what would you say? Go on.

ZACHARIAH. Cookie . . . or . . . Bokkie . . .

MORRIS. (*quickly*) You're getting hot, but that, Zach, is what we call a personal address, but you only use it later. This time you say: Dear Ethel.

ZACHARIAH. Just like that?

MORRIS. You get her on friendly terms. Now comes the introduction. (*writes*) "With reply to your advert for a pen-pal, I hereby write." (*holds up the writing paper*) Taking shape, hey! Now tell her who you are and where you are.

ZACHARIAH. How?

MORRIS. I am . . . and so on.

ZACHARIAH. I am Zach and I . . .

MORRIS. . . . ariah Pietersen . . . go on.

ZACHARIAH. And I am at Korsten.

MORRIS. As you will see from the above.

ZACHARIAH. What's that?

MORRIS. Something you must add in letters. (*newspaper*) She says here: My interests are nature, rock-and-roll, swimming and a happy future. Well, what do you say to that?

ZACHARIAH. Shit! (*pause, frozen stare from MORRIS*) Sorry, Morrie. Nature and a happy future. Ja. Good luck! How's that? Good luck, Ethel.

MORRIS. Not bad. A little short, though. How about: I notice your plans, and wish you good luck with them.

ZACHARIAH. Sure, sure. Put that there.

MORRIS. (*He writes, then returns to the newspaper.*) "My motto is' 'rolling stones gather no moss.' (*pause*) That's tricky. Wait! I have it! How do you feel about: "Too many cooks spoil the broth." That's my favourite.

ZACHARIAH. Why not? Why not, I ask?

MORRIS. (*writes*) "Experience has taught me to make my motto: 'Too many cooks spoil the broth.'" Now let's get a bit general, Zach.

ZACHARIAH. (*yawning*) Just as you say.

MORRIS. (*after a pause*) Well, it's your letter. (*not fooled by the feigned interest, pause*) I can make a suggestion.

ZACHARIAH. That's fine. Put that down there, too.

MORRIS. No, Zach. (*MORRIS writes.*)

ZACHARIAH. How about I'd like to see you too. Send me a photo.

MORRIS. . . . please . . . I'm near the bottom now. Please write soon. Yours . . .

ZACHARIAH. Hers?

MORRIS. . . . faithfully. Zachariah Pietersen. (*ZACHARIAH prepares for bed. MORRIS addresses and seals the envelope.*) I'll get this off tomorrow. Remember, this is your letter, and what comes back is going to be your reply.

ZACHARIAH. And yours?

MORRIS. Mine?

ZACHARIAH. There's still Nellie. Or Betty. (*Alarm rings. ZACHARIAH flops back on his bed laughing. MORRIS drifts to the window.*)

MORRIS. Wind's coming up. You sleepy?

ZACHARIAH. It's been a long day.

MORRIS. Okay, we'll cut it short. (*MORRIS fetches a Bible from the shelf over his bed.*)

ZACHARIAH. No, Morrie, you say it tonight. (*MORRIS kneels. ZACHARIAH follows suit.*)

MORRIS. Give thanks to God for those who love you — and who you love. Ask for what you most want.

ZACHARIAH. Dear God, please bring back Minnie.

MORRIS. Is that all? Zach? Amen. (*He replaces the Bible, finds needle and cotton and then takes ZACHARIAH's coat to the table.*) I'm helping you, aren't I, Zach?

ZACHARIAH. Ja.

MORRIS. I want to believe that. You see . . . (*pause*) there was all those years, when I was away.

ZACHARIAH. Why did you come back?

MORRIS. I was passing this way.

ZACHARIAH. Why did you stay?

MORRIS. We are brothers, remember. (*A few seconds pass in silence. MORRIS threads his needle and then starts working on a tear in ZACHARIAH's coat.*) That's a word, hey! Brothers! There's a broody sound

for you if ever there was. I mean . . . Take the others.
Father. What is there for us in . . . Father? We never
knew him. Even Mother. She died and we were young.
That's the trouble with "Mother." We never said it
enough. (*He tries it.*) Mother. Mother! Yes. Just a
touch of sadness in it, and maybe a grey dress on Sundays, and soapsuds on brown hands. That's the lot. Father, Mother, and the sisters we haven't got. But
brothers! Try it. Brotherhood. Brother-in-arms, each
other's arms. Brotherly love. Zach? (*He looks at
ZACHARIAH's bed.*) Zachie? Zachariah! (*He is
asleep. MORRIS takes the lamp, goes to the bed and
looks down at the sleeping man. He returns to the table,
picks up the Bible and after an inward struggle speaks in
a solemn, "Sunday" voice.*) "And he said: What hast
thou done? The voice of thy brother's blood crieth unto
me!" (*MORRIS drops his head in an admission of
guilt.*) Maybe he needs you. You better go home, man!
(*pause*) So he turned around on the road, and came
back. About this time, a year ago. I thought: it looks the
same. It was. Because when I reached the first pondok-
kies and the thin dogs, the wind turned and brought the
stink from the lake. No one recognized me. I could see
they weren't sure, and wanting to say Sir when I asked
them the way. Six down, they said, pointing to the
water's edge. So then there was only time left for a few,
short thoughts between counting doors. Will he be
home? Will I be welcome? Be forgiven? Be brave, Morris! I held my breath . . . and knocked . . . and waited
. . . and his steps beyond the door . . . (*pause*) You
were wearing this coat . . . and that night, when you
slept, I put it on . . . I've got to get to know him again, I
said, this brother of mine, all over again. (*MORRIS
puts on ZACHARIAH's coat. It is several sizes too*

large.) You get right inside the man when you can wrap-up in the smell of him. It's been a big help to me. It prepared me for your flesh, Zach. Because your flesh, you see, has an effect on me. The sight of it, the feel of it . . . I saw you again after all those years . . . and it hurt.

ACT TWO

SCENE 1

A few days later. MORRIS is at the table counting their savings—banknotes and silver. The alarm clock rings. He sweeps the money into a tin which he then carefully hides among the pots on the kitchen-dresser. Next he resets the clock and prepares the footbath as in the first scene. ZACHARIAH appears, silent and sullen, goes straight to the bed, where he sits.

MORRIS. You look tired tonight, old fellow. (*ZACHARIAH looks at him askance.*) Today too long? I'd say that's a weary body. Am I right, old fellow?

ZACHARIAH. What's this "old fellow" thing you got hold of tonight?

MORRIS. Just a figure of speaking, Zach. The Englishman would say "old boy" . . . but we don't like that "boy" business, hey?

ZACHARIAH. Ja. They call a man a boy. You got a word for that, Morrie?

MORRIS. Long or short?

ZACHARIAH. Squashed, like it didn't fit the mouth.

MORRIS. I know the one you mean.

ZACHARIAH. Then say it.

MORRIS. Prejudice.

ZACHARIAH. Pre-ja-dis.

MORRIS. Injustice!

ZACHARIAH. That's all out of shape as well.

MORRIS. Inhumanity!

29

ZACHARIAH. No. That's when he makes me stand at the gate.

MORRIS. Am I right in thinking you were there again today?

ZACHARIAH. All day long.

MORRIS. You tried to go back to the pots?

ZACHARIAH. I tried to go back to the pots. My feet, I said, are killing me.

MORRIS. And then?

ZACHARIAH. Go to the gate or go to hell . . . Boy!

MORRIS. He said boy as well?

ZACHARIAH. He did.

MORRIS. In one sentence?

ZACHARIAH. Prejudice and inhumanity in one sentence! (*He starts to work off one shoe with the other foot and then dips the bare foot into the basin of water. He will not get as far as taking off the other shoe.*) When your feet are bad, you feel it. (*MORRIS starts helping ZACHARIAH take off his coat. At this point MORRIS finds an envelope in the inside pocket of ZACHARIAH's coat. He examines it secretly. ZACHARIAH broods on, one foot in the basin.*)

MORRIS. Did you stop by the Post Office on your way back?

ZACHARIAH. Ja. There was a letter.

MORRIS. I know there was. (*holding up the envelope*) I just found it.

ZACHARIAH. Good.

MORRIS. Good? What do you mean good?

ZACHARIAH. You know . . . good, like okay.

MORRIS. (*excited and annoyed*) What's the matter with you? Don't you realize? This is your pen-pal. This is your reply from Ethel!

ZACHARIAH. In Oudtshoorn.

MORRIS. But Zach! You must get excited, man! Don't you want to know what she said?

ZACHARIAH. Sure.

MORRIS. Shall we open it then?

ZACHARIAH. Why not!

MORRIS. (*He tears open the letter.*) By God, she did it! She sent you a picture of herself.

ZACHARIAH. (*first flicker of interest*) She did?

MORRIS. So this is Ethel!

ZACHARIAH. Morrie. . . ?

MORRIS. Eighteen years . . . and fully . . . developed.

ZACHARIAH. Let me see, man! (*He grabs the photograph. The certainty and excitement fade from MORRIS' face. He is obviously perplexed at something.*) Hey! Not bad. Now that's what I call a goosie. Good for old Oudtshoorn, I say. You don't get them like this over here. That I can tell you. Not with a watch! You see that, Morrie. Good for old Ethel, all right. Pretty smart, too. Nice hair. Just look at those locks. And how's that for a wall she's standing against. Ever seen a wall like that, as big as that, in Korsten? I mean it's made of bricks, isn't it!

MORRIS. (*snatching the photograph out of ZACHARIAH's and taking it to the window where he has a good look*) Give it to me!

ZACHARIAH. Hey! What's the matter with you! It's my pen-pal, isn't it? It is!

MORRIS. Keep quiet, Zach!

ZACHARIAH. What's this "keep quiet"? It's my room, isn't it? It is!

MORRIS. Where's the letter?

ZACHARIAH. You had it.

MORRIS. Where did I put it? (*He throws the photograph down on the bed and finds the letter, which he reads feverishly. ZACHARIAH picks up the photograph and continues his study.*)

ZACHARIAH. You're acting like you never seen a woman in your life. Why don't you get a pen-pal? Maybe one's not enough.

MORRIS. (*Having finished the letter, his agitation is now even more pronounced.*) That newspaper, Zach. Where is the newspaper?

ZACHARIAH. How should I know?

MORRIS. (*anguish*) Think, man!

ZACHARIAH. You had it. (*MORRIS is scratching around frantically.*) What's the matter with you tonight? Maybe you threw it away.

MORRIS. No. I was keeping it in case . . . (*finds it*) Thank God! Oh, please, God, now make it that I am wrong!

ZACHARIAH. What the hell are you talking about?

MORRIS. (*He takes a look at the newspaper, pages through it and then drops it. He stands quite still, unnaturally calm after the frenzy of the previous few seconds.*) You know what you done, don't you?

ZACHARIAH. Me?

MORRIS. Who was it then? Me? Who wanted woman?

ZACHARIAH. Me.

MORRIS. Right. Who's been carrying on about Minnie, and Connie, and good times? Not me.

ZACHARIAH. Morrie! What are you talking about?

MORRIS. That photograph.

ZACHARIAH. I've seen it.

MORRIS. Well, have another look.

ZACHARIAH. (*He does.*) It's Ethel.

MORRIS. *Miss* Ethel Lange to you!

ZACHARIAH. Okay, I looked. Now what?

MORRIS. Can't you see, man! Ethel Lange is a white woman! (*Pause. They look at each other in silence.*)

ZACHARIAH. (*slowly*) You mean that this Ethel . . . here . . .

MORRIS. Is a white woman!

ZACHARIAH. How do you know?

MORRIS. Use your eyes. Those papers you brought home is white. There's no news about our sort.

ZACHARIAH. (*studying the photo*) You're right, Morrie. (*delighted*) You're damn well right. And she's written to me, to a hotnot, a swartgat. This white woman thinks I'm a white man. That I like! (*ZACHARIAH bursts into laughter. MORRIS jumps forward and snatches the photograph out of his hand.*) Hey! What you going to do?

MORRIS. What do you think?

ZACHARIAH. Read it.

MORRIS. I'm going to burn it.

ZACHARIAH. No!

MORRIS. Yes.

ZACHARIAH. I say no! (*ZACHARIAH jumps up and comes to grips with MORRIS who, after a short struggle, is thrown violently to the floor. ZACHARIAH picks up the letter and the photograph. He stands looking down at MORRIS for a few seconds, amazed at what he has done.*) You're not going to burn it.

MORRIS. You knocked me down.

ZACHARIAH. You was going to burn it.

MORRIS. (*vehemently*) Yes, burn it! Destroy it!

ZACHARIAH. But it's my pen-pal, Morris. Now, isn't it? Doesn't it say here: Mr. Zachariah Pietersen? Well, that's me . . . isn't it? It is. My letter. You just don't go and burn another man's letter, Morrie.

MORRIS. But it's an error, Zach! Can't you see? The whole thing is an error.

ZACHARIAH. You must read it to me first. I don't know. (*The alarm rings.*)

MORRIS. Supper time.

ZACHARIAH. Later.

MORRIS. Listen—

ZACHARIAH. Letter first.

MORRIS. Then can I burn it?

ZACHARIAH. Read the letter first, man. Let's hear it. (*handing MORRIS the letter*) No funny business, hey!

MORRIS. (*reading*) "Dear Zach, many thanks for your letter. You asked me for a snap, so I'm sending you it. Do you like it? That's my brother's foot sticking in the picture behind the bench on the side—"

ZACHARIAH. She's right! Here it is.

MORRIS. "Cornelius is a . . . policeman." (*pause*)

ZACHARIAH. (*serene*) Go on.

MORRIS. "He's got a motor-bike, and I been with him to the dam, on the back. My best friend is Lucy van Tonder. Both of us hates Oudtshoorn, man. How is P.E.? There's only two bios here, so we don't know what to do on the other nights. That's why I want pen-pals. How about a . . . picture . . ." (*pause*)

ZACHARIAH. (*still serenely confident*) Go on.

MORRIS. "How about a picture of you? You got a car? All for now. Tot siens, Ethel. P.S. Please write soon." (*MORRIS folds the letter.*) Satisfied?

ZACHARIAH. (*gratefully*) Thank you, Morrie. (*holds out his hand for the letter*)

MORRIS. Can I burn it now?

ZACHARIAH. Burn it! It's an all-right letter, man. A little bit of this and a little bit of that.

MORRIS. Like her brother being a policeman.

ZACHARIAH. (*ignoring the last remark*) Supper ready yet? Let's talk after supper, man. I'm hungry. What you got, Morrie?

MORRIS. Boiled eggs and chips.

ZACHARIAH. Sounds good. Hey! We never had that before.

MORRIS. (*sulking*) It was meant to be a surprise.

ZACHARIAH. But that's wonderful. (*ZACHARIAH is full of vigour and life.*) No, I mean it, Morrie. Cross my heart, and hope to die. Boiled egg! I never even knew you could do it. (*ZACHARIAH takes his place at the table, and stands the photograph in front of him. When MORRIS brings the food to the table, he sees it and hesitates.*) Just looking, Morrie. She sent it for me to look at, didn't she? (*Eats. MORRIS sits down.*) What's it got here on the back?

MORRIS. (*examines the back of the photograph*) "To Zach, with love, from Ethel."

(*Another burst of laughter from ZACHARIAH. MORRIS leaves the table abruptly.*)

ZACHARIAH. (*calmly continuing with his meal*) What's the matter?

MORRIS. I'm not hungry.

ZACHARIAH. You mean, you don't like to hear me laugh?

MORRIS. It's not that . . .

ZACHARIAH. It is. But it's funny, man. She and me. Of course, it wouldn't be so funny if it was you who was pally with her.

MORRIS. What does that mean?

ZACHARIAH. Don't you know?

MORRIS. No. So will you kindly please tell me?

ZACHARIAH. You never seen yourself, Morrie?

MORRIS. (*trembling with emotion*) Be careful, Zach! I'm warning you now. Just be careful of where your words are taking you!

ZACHARIAH. Okay. Okay. (*eats in silence*) You was telling me the other day about Oudtshoorn. How far you say it was?

MORRIS. (*viciously*) Hundreds of miles.

ZACHARIAH. So far, hey?

MORRIS. Don't fool yourself. It's *not* far enough for safety's sake. Cornelius has got a motorbike, remember.

ZACHARIAH. Ja. But we don't write to him, man.

MORRIS. Listen, Zach, if you think for one moment that I'm going to write . . .

ZACHARIAH. Think? Who says? I been eating my supper. It was good, Morrie. The eggs and chips. Tasty.

MORRIS. Don't try to change the subject matter!

ZACHARIAH. Me? I like that. You mean, what's the matter with you! You was the one that spoke about pen-pals first. Not me.

MORRIS. So here it comes at last. I've been waiting for it. I'm to blame, am I? All right. I'll take the blame. I always did, didn't I? But this is where it ends. I'm telling you now, burn that letter, because when they come around here and ask me, I'll say I got nothing more to do with it.

ZACHARIAH. Burn this letter! What's wrong with this letter?

MORRIS. Ethel Lange is a white woman!

ZACHARIAH. Wait . . . wait . . . wait . . . not so fast. I'm a sort of slow man. Now tell me, what's wrong with what you did read? Does she call me names? No. Does she laugh at me? No. Does she swear at me? No. Just a simple letter with a little bit of this and a little bit of that. What sort of chap is it that throws away a few kind words? Hey, Morrie? Aren't they, as you say, precious things these days? And this pretty picture of a lovely girl? I burn it! What sort of doing is that? Bad. Think of

Ethel, man. Think! Sitting up there in Oudtshoorn with Lucy, waiting . . . waiting . . . for what? For nothing. For why? Because bad Zach Pietersen burnt it.

MORRIS. (*pause*) I just want to remind you, Zach, that when I was writing to her you weren't even interested in a single thing I said. But now, suddenly, now you are! Why? Why, I ask myself . . . and a suspicious little voice answers: is it maybe because she's white?

ZACHARIAH. Okay. Do you want to hear me say it? (*MORRIS says nothing.*) It's because she's white! I like this little white girl! I like the thought of this little white girl. I'm telling you I like the thought of this little white Ethel better than our future, or the plans, or getting away, or foot salts or any other damned thing in here. It's the best thought I ever had and I'm keeping it, and don't you try no tricks like trying to get it away from me. Who knows? You might get to liking it too. (*MORRIS says nothing. ZACHARIAH comes closer.*) Ja. There's a thought there. What about *you,* Morrie? You never had it before—that thought? A man like you, specially you, always thinking so many things! A man like you who's been places! You're always telling me about the places you been. Wasn't there ever no white woman thereabouts? I mean . . . You must have smelt them someplace. That sweet, white smell, you know. (*nudging MORRIS*) Of course, you did. Hey? I bet you had that thought all the time. I bet you been having it in here. Hey? You should have shared it, Morrie. I'm a man with a taste for thoughts these days. It hurts to think you didn't share a good one like that with your brother. Giving me all that shit about future and plans, and then keeping the real goosie for yourself. You weren't scared, were you? That I would tell? You were scared, hey! A little bit poopy. I've noticed that. But you needn't worry now. I'm a man for keeping a secret, and anyway, we'll play this very careful . . . very, very careful. Ethel won't never know about us, and I know how to handle that brother. Mustn't let a policeman bugger you about, man. So, let's go get your pencil and piece of paper. (*MORRIS is defeated. He sits at the table. ZACHARIAH paces.*) So we'll take her on friendly terms again. (*pause*) "Dear Ethel." (*MORRIS writes.*) "I think you might like to know I got your letter, and the picture. I'd say Oudtshoorn seems all right. You were quite all right too. I would like to send you a picture of me, but it's this way. It's winter down here now. The light is bad, the lake is black, the birds have gone. Wait for spring, when things improve. Okay? Good. I heard you ask about my car. Yes. I have it. We pumped the tyres today. Tomorrow I think I'll put in some petrol. I'd like to take you for a drive, Ethel and Lucy too. In fact, I'd like to drive both of you. They say over here, I'm fast. I'll tell you this. If I could drive you, I would do it so fast, Ethel, and Lucy too, both of you, so fast I would, it would hurt—"

MORRIS. Okay, Zach!

ZACHARIAH. (*pulling himself together*) "Ja! But don't worry. I got brakes." (*pause*) "I notice your brother got boots. All policemen got boots, I notice. Good luck to him, anyway, and Lucy too. Write soon. Zachariah Pietersen." (*pause*) Okay, Morrie. Do your business on the envelope, but I'll post it. There, you see! Nothing to it, was there? A little bit of this and a little bit of that and nothing about some things. When Ethel gets it she'll say: "He's okay. This Zachariah Pietersen is okay, Lucy!"

MORRIS. I have a feeling about it.

ZACHARIAH. A feeling about Ethel? (*laughs*) I told you.

MORRIS. Zach! (*pause*) Let me burn it.

ZACHARIAH. My letter?

MORRIS. Yes.

ZACHARIAH. The one we just done?

MORRIS. Yes.

ZACHARIAH. Ethel's letter, now my letter! (*He gets up and takes the letter in question away from MORRIS.*) You're in a burning mood, all right.

MORRIS. Please, Zach. You're going to get hurt.

ZACHARIAH. (*aggression*) Such as by who?

MORRIS. Ethel. (*ZACHARIAH laughs.*) That. There in your hand. To Miss Ethel Lange. You think that's a letter? I'm telling you it's a drea, and the most dangerous one. That's what they call evidence, you know. (*pause*) God, Zach, I have a feeling about this business, man!

ZACHARIAH. Cheer up, Morrie. Like you said, it's just a game.

MORRIS. But you're playing with fire, Zach. It's an awful game.

ZACHARIAH. Maybe. But then I never had much to play with.

MORRIS. Didn't you?

ZACHARIAH. Don't you remember? You got the toys.

MORRIS. Did I?

ZACHARIAH. Ja. Like that top, Morrie. I have always remembered that brown stinkwood top. She gave me her old cotton reels to play with, but it wasn't the same. I wanted a top.

MORRIS. Who? Who gave me the top?

ZACHARIAH. Mother.

MORRIS. Mother!

ZACHARIAH. Ja. She said she only had one. There was always only one.

MORRIS. Zach, you're telling me a thing now!

ZACHARIAH. Did you forget her?

MORRIS. No, Zach. I meant the top. I can't remember that top. And what about her, Zach? There's a memory for you. I tried it out the other day. Mother, I said, Mother! A sadness, I thought.

ZACHARIAH. Remember her feet. (*Pause. MORRIS looks at ZACHARIAH.*)

MORRIS. What do you mean?

ZACHARIAH. There were her feet.

MORRIS. Who had feet?

ZACHARIAH. Mother, man.

MORRIS. I don't remember her feet, Zach.

ZACHARIAH. (*serenely confident*) Ja, man. The toes were crooked, the nails skew and there was pain. They didn't fit the shoes.

MORRIS. (*growing agitation*) Zach, are you sure there wasn't somebody else?

ZACHARIAH. She let me feel the hardness and then pruned them down with a razor blade.

MORRIS. No, Zach. You got me worried now! A grey dress?

ZACHARIAH. Maybe.

MORRIS. (*persistent*) Going to church. She wore it going to —

ZACHARIAH. The butcher shop! That's it! That's where she went.

MORRIS. Stop, Zach. Stop! We must sort this out, man. I mean . . . It sounds like some other mother.

ZACHARIAH. (*gently*) How can that be?

MORRIS. Listen, Zach. Do you remember the songs she sang?

ZACHARIAH. Do I! (*He laughs and then sings:*)
My skin is black,
The soap is blue,
But the washing comes out white.

I took a man
On a Friday night;
Now I'm washing a baby too.

Just a little bit black,
And a little bit white,
He's a Capie through and through.
(*MORRIS is staring at him in horror.*) What's the matter?

MORRIS. That wasn't what she sang to me. (*anguish*) This is terrible. What . . . wait! I've got it . . . I think. Oh, God, let it be that I've got it. (*to ZACHARIAH*) How about the games we played? Think, Zach. Think carefully! There was one special one. Just me and you. I'll give you a clue. Toot-toot. Toot-toot.

ZACHARIAH. (*thinking*) Wasn't there an old car?

MORRIS. Where would it be?

ZACHARIAH. Rusting by the side of the road.

MORRIS. Could it be the ruins of an old Chevy, Zach?

ZACHARIAH. It could.

MORRIS. And can we say with tyres and wires and things?

ZACHARIAH. We may.

MORRIS. . . . and all the glass blown away by the wind?

ZACHARIAH. Dusty.

MORRIS. Deserted.

ZACHARIAH. Sting bees on the bonnet.

MORRIS. Webs in the windscreen.

ZACHARIAH. Nothing in the boot.

MORRIS. And us?

ZACHARIAH. In it.

MORRIS. We arc? How?

ZACHARIAH. Side by side.

MORRIS. Like this? (*He sits beside ZACHARIAH.*)

ZACHARIAH. That's right.

MORRIS. Doing what?

ZACHARIAH. Staring.

MORRIS. Not both of us!

ZACHARIAH. Me at the wheel, you at the window.

MORRIS. Okay. Now what?

ZACHARIAH. Now, I got this gear here and I'm going to go.

MORRIS. Where?

ZACHARIAH. To hell and gone far away, and we aren't coming back.

MORRIS. Wait! What will I do while you drive?

ZACHARIAH. You must tell me what we pass. Are you ready? Here we go! (*ZACHARIAH goes through the motions of driving a car. MORRIS looks eagerly out of the window.*)

MORRIS. We're slipping through the streets, passing homes and people on the pavements who are quite friendly and wave as we drive by. It's a fine, sunny sort of a day. What are we doing?

ZACHARIAH. Twenty-four.

MORRIS. Do you see that bus ahead of us? (*They lean over to one side as ZACHARIAH swings the wheel. MORRIS looks back.*) Chock-a-block with early morning workers. Shame. And what about those children over there, going to school? Shame again. On such a nice day. What are we doing?

ZACHARIAH. Thirty-four.

MORRIS. That means we're coming to open country. The white houses have given way to patches of green and animals and not so many people anymore. But they still wave . . . with their spades.

ZACHARIAH. Fifty.

MORRIS. You're going quite fast. You've killed a cat, flattened a frog, frightened a dog . . . who jumped!

ZACHARIAH. Sixty.

MORRIS. Passing trees, and haystacks, and sunshine and the smoke from little houses drifting by . . . shooting by!

ZACHARIAH. Eighty!

MORRIS. Birds flying abreast, and bulls, billygoats, black sheep . . .

ZACHARIAH. One hundred!

MORRIS. . . . cross a river, up a hill, to the top, coming down, down, down . . . stop! stop!

ZACHARIAH. (*slamming on the brakes*) Eeeee-ooooooooaah! (*pause*) Why?

MORRIS. Look! There's a butterfly.

ZACHARIAH. On your side?

MORRIS. Yours as well. Just look.

ZACHARIAH. All around us, hey!

MORRIS. This is rare, Zach! We've driven into a flock of butterflies. (*ZACHARIAH smiles and then laughs.*) We've found it, Zach. We've found it! This is our youth!

ZACHARIAH. And driving to hell and gone was our game.

MORRIS. Our best one. And the trees! Me and you in the trees, Zach. Tarzan and his ape. My God! The things a man can forget!

ZACHARIAH. Ja. Those were the days!

MORRIS. God knows!

ZACHARIAH. What's that . . . that . . . that nice song, Morrie?

MORRIS.
"So sweet did pass that summer time,

Of youth and fruit upon the trees,
When laughing boys and pretty girls
Did hop and skip and all were free."

ZACHARIAH. Did skop and skip the pretty girls. They did, too.

MORRIS. We played our games, Zach. (*pause*) There were a few falls of course. A few inner hurts, too.

ZACHARIAH. What was those?

MORRIS. Don't you remember? Kaffertjie, Kaffertjie, waar is jou pas?

ZACHARIAH. (*taking up the jingle*) But my old man was a white man.

MORRIS.
Maar, jou ma was 'n Bantoe,
So dis nou jou ras.

ZACHARIAH. (*shaking his head*) Ja. That hurt.

MORRIS. But on the whole it was fun.

ZACHARIAH. While it lasted, which wasn't for long.

MORRIS. It had to happen, Zach. We grew up, mother lay down and died, so I went away. (*pause*) Here we are, later. And now there's Ethel as well, and that makes me frightened.

ZACHARIAH. Sounds like another game, hey?

MORRIS. Yes. But not ours . . . this time. (*They sit together, overshadowed by the presence in their words.*)

SCENE 2

An evening later. ZACHARIAH is seated at the table, eating. He is obviously in good spirits, radiating an inward satisfaction and secrecy. MORRIS is moving about nervously behind his back.

MORRIS. So. Do you want to tell me?

ZACHARIAH. What are you talking about, Morrie?

MORRIS. You got a letter today, didn't you?

ZACHARIAH. Who?

MORRIS. You.

ZACHARIAH. What?

MORRIS. A letter. From Ethel. And you're not telling me about it. (*ZACHARIAH continues eating, unaffected by MORRIS' words.*) Come on now, Zach. You did, didn't you? Same sort as usual? (*ZACHARIAH looks at MORRIS.*) The letter. (*ZACHARIAH puts down his bread and thinks. MORRIS seizes his opportunity.*) Didn't you notice? Hell, Zach! You surprise me.

ZACHARIAH. What do you mean: the same sort?

MORRIS. To begin with there's the . . . envelope. Is it the same colour, or isn't it? I can see that somebody didn't take a good look, did he? (*Reluctantly ZACHARIAH takes the letter out of his inside pocket.*) She's changed her colours! They used to be blue. What about inside?

ZACHARIAH. I'm not ready for that yet.

MORRIS. Okay. All I'm saying is . . . I don't care.

ZACHARIAH. (*studying the envelope*) I see they got animals on stamps nowadays. The donkeys with stripes.

MORRIS. Zebras.

ZACHARIAH. . . . with stripes.

MORRIS. That's not the point about a letter, Zach.

ZACHARIAH. What?

MORRIS. The stamps. You're wasting your time with the stamps. It's what's inside that you got to read.

ZACHARIAH. You're in a hurry, Morrie.

MORRIS. Who?

ZACHARIAH. You.

MORRIS. Look, I told you that all I'm saying is . . . I don't care and the stamps don't count. Other than that, have your fun. It means nothing to me.

ZACHARIAH. And my name on the envelope. How do you like that, hey?

MORRIS. *Your* name?

ZACHARIAH. Ja. My name.

MORRIS. Oh.

ZACHARIAH. Now what do you mean, with an "Oh" like that?

MORRIS. What makes you so sure that that is your name? (*ZACHARIAH is trapped.*) How do you spell your name, Zach? Come on, let's hear.

ZACHARIAH. (*after a long struggle*) Zach . . . ah . . . ri . . . yah.

MORRIS. Oh, no, you don't! That's no spelling. That's a pronunciation. A b c d e . . . that's the alphabet. (*After a moment's hesitation, ZACHARIAH holds up the letter so that MORRIS can see the address.*)

ZACHARIAH. Is it for me, Morrie?

MORRIS. I'm not sure.

ZACHARIAH. Mr. Zachariah Pietersen.

MORRIS. I know your name. It's for one Z. Pietersen.

ZACHARIAH. Well, that's okay then.

MORRIS. Is it?

ZACHARIAH. Isn't it?

MORRIS. Since when are you the only thing that begins with a Z?

ZACHARIAH. (*He keeps the letter for a few more seconds, then hands it to MORRIS.*) You win. Read it.

MORRIS. I win! (*laughs happily, nudging ZACH-ARIAH*) It pays to have a brother who can read, hey? (*opens the letter*) Ready? "Dear Zach, How's things?

I'm okay, today, again. I got your letter . . ." (*continues his reading*) "Lucy had a laugh at you, but my brother is not so sure." (*pause*) That, I feel, means something. What does it do to you?

ZACHARIAH. Nothing.

MORRIS. (*He reads on.*) "I'm looking forward to a ride in your car . . ." They believed it, Zach! (*ZACHARIAH smiles.*) They believed your cock and bull about the car.

ZACHARIAH. (*laughing*) I told you.

MORRIS. "I'm looking forward to a ride in your car . . . and what about Lucy? Can she come?" (*Their amusement knows no bounds.*)

ZACHARIAH. You must come too, Morrie. You and Lucy! Hey! We'll take them at ninety.

MORRIS. (*reads on through his laughter*) "We're coming down for a holiday in June, so where . . . can we . . . meet you?" (*Long pause. He reads again.*) "We're coming down for a holiday in June so where can we meet you?"

ZACHARIAH. Ethel . . . ?

MORRIS. Is coming here. (*puts down the letter and stands up*) I warned you, didn't I? I said: I have a feeling about this business. I told you to leave it alone. Hands off! Don't touch! But, oh, no, Mr. Z. Pietersen was clever. He knew how to handle it. Well, handle this, will you please?

ZACHARIAH. (*dumbly*) What else does she say?

MORRIS. (*brutally*) I'm not going to read it. You want to know why? Because it doesn't matter. The game's up, man. Nothing else matters now except: "I'm coming down in June so where can we meet you?" That is what Mr. Z. Pietersen had better start thinking about . . . and quick!

ZACHARIAH. When's June?

MORRIS. Soon.

ZACHARIAH. How soon?

MORRIS. Look. Are you trying to make me out a liar? (*ticking them off on his fingers*) January, February, March, April, May, June, July, August, September, October, November, December? Satisfied? (*Another long pause. MORRIS goes back to the window.*)

ZACHARIAH. So?

MORRIS. (*to the table, where he reads further into the letter*) "I'll be staying with my uncle at Kensington." (*little laugh*) Kensington! Near enough for you? About five minutes walking from here, hey? . . . with my uncle. Uncle!

ZACHARIAH. (*He is frightened.*) Morrie, I know. I'll tell her I can't see her.

MORRIS. She will want to know why.

ZACHARIAH. It's because I'm sick, with my heart.

MORRIS. And if she feels sorry and comes to comfort you.

ZACHARIAH. (*growing desperation*) But I'm going away.

MORRIS. When?

ZACHARIAH. Soon. June.

MORRIS. And what about where, and why and what, if she says she'll wait until you come back?

ZACHARIAH. Then I'll tell her . . . (*Pause. He can think of nothing else to say.*)

MORRIS. Tell her what? You can't even tell her you're dead. You see, I happen to know. There is not white-washing away a man's facts. They'll speak for themselves at first sight, if you don't say it.

ZACHARIAH. Say what?

MORRIS. The truth. You know it.

ZACHARIAH. I don't. I don't know nothing.

MORRIS. Then listen, because *I* know it. "Dear Ethel, forgive me, but I was born a dark sort of boy who wanted to play with whiteness . . ."

ZACHARIAH. (*rebelling*) No!

MORRIS. Then tell me what else you can say? Come one. Let's hear it.

ZACHARIAH. There must be something.

MORRIS. I'm telling you there's nothing . . . there is only the truth and . . . (*He pauses.*)

ZACHARIAH. And then what?

MORRIS. And then to make a run for it. They don't like these games with their whiteness. Ethel's got a policeman brother and an uncle and *your* address.

ZACHARIAH. What have I done, hey? I done nothing.

MORRIS. What have you thought! That's the crime. I seem to remember somebody saying: "I like the thought of this little white girl." When they get their hands on a dark-born boy playing with a white idea, you think they don't find out what he's been dreaming at night? They have ways and means, my friend. Mean ways. Like confinement, in a cell, on bread and water, for days without end. They got time. All they need of evidence is a man's dreams. Not so much his hate. They say they can live with that. It's his dreams that they drag off to judgment, shouting: "Silence! He's been caught! He's guilty! Take him away." (*pause*) Where? You know where, Zach. You've seen them, in the streets, carrying their spades and the man with his gun. Bald heads, short trousers and that ugly jersey with the red, painful stripes around the body. (*MORRIS goes back to the window.*) I miss the moths. They made the night a friendly sort of place. (*turning to ZACHARIAH*) What are you going to do about it, Zach?

ZACHARIAH. I'm thinking about it.

MORRIS. What are you thinking about it?

ZACHARIAH. What am I going to do? Help me, Morrie.

MORRIS. Let's go. Begin at the beginning. Give me the first fact.

ZACHARIAH. (*severe and bitter*) Ethel is white. I am black.

MORRIS. That's a very good beginning, Zach.

ZACHARIAH. If she sees me . . .

MORRIS. Keep it up.

ZACHARIAH. . . . she'll be surprised.

MORRIS. Harder, Zach.

ZACHARIAH. She'll laugh.

MORRIS. Let it hurt, man! Worse—

ZACHARIAH. She'll scream!

MORRIS. Good! Now for yourself. She's surprised, remember?

ZACHARIAH. I'm not strange.

MORRIS. And when she swears?

ZACHARIAH. I'm no dog.

MORRIS. She screams!

ZACHARIAH. I just wanted to smell you, lady!

MORRIS. Good, Zach. Very good. But, remember there is still the others.

ZACHARIAH. What others?

MORRIS. The uncles with fists as big as my head and policemen brothers in boots.

ZACHARIAH. What about them?

MORRIS. They've come to ransack you.

ZACHARIAH. I'll say it wasn't me.

MORRIS. They won't believe you.

ZACHARIAH. Leave me alone!

MORRIS. They'll hit you for that.

ZACHARIAH. I'll fight.

MORRIS. There's too many for you.

ZACHARIAH. I'll call a policeman.

MORRIS. He's on their side.

ZACHARIAH. I'll run away!

MORRIS. That's better. Go back to the beginning. (*pause*) It started with Ethel, remember. Ethel . . .

ZACHARIAH. . . . is white.

MORRIS. That's it. And . . .

ZACHARIAH. . . . and I am black. Ethel is white and I am black. Ethel is so . . . so . . . snow white.

MORRIS. And . . . come on . . .

ZACHARIAH. And I am too . . . truly . . . too black.

MORRIS. Now, this is the hard part, Zach. I'm with you all the way, remember, just this one cry and then never again . . . and, as they say, tomorrow is another, yet another day, and a man must carry on. Doesn't matter so much where; just on, just carry on . . . let's hear it, Zach.

ZACHARIAH. I can never have her.

MORRIS. Never ever.

ZACHARIAH. She wouldn't want me anyway.

MORRIS. It's as simple as that.

ZACHARIAH. She's too white to want me anyway.

MORRIS. For better or for worse.

ZACHARIAH. So I won't want her anymore.

MORRIS. Not in this life, or if death us do part, that next one, God help us! For ever and ever no more, thank you!

ZACHARIAH. The whole, rotten, stinking lot is all because I'm black! I'm black all right. Black days, black ways, black things. They're me. I'm happy. Ha Ha Ha! Do you hear my black happiness?

MORRIS. Oh, yes, Zach, I hear it, I promise you.

ZACHARIAH. Can you feel it?

MORRIS. I do. I do.

ZACHARIAH. I'm on my side, they're on theirs. Because from now on, I'll be what I am.

MORRIS. (*quietly, and with absolute sincerity*) Zach! Oh, Zach! When I hear that certainty about whys and wherefores, about how to live and what not to love, I wish, believe me, deep down in the bottom of my heart where my blood is as red as yours, I wish that old washerwoman had bruised me too at birth. I wish— (*The alarm goes off. MORRIS looks up to find ZACHARIAH staring strangely at him. MORRIS goes to the window to avoid ZACHARIAH's eyes. He turns from the window to find ZACHARIAH still staring at him. MORRIS goes to the table to turn off the lamp.*)

ZACHARIAH. Morris!

MORRIS. Zachariah?

ZACHARIAH. Keep on the light.

MORRIS. Why?

ZACHARIAH. I saw something.

MORRIS. What?

ZACHARIAH. Your skin. How can I put it? It's . . . (*pause*)

MORRIS. (*easily*) On the light side.

ZACHARIAH. Ja.

MORRIS. (*very easily*) One of those things. (*another move to the lamp*)

ZACHARIAH. Wait, Morrie!

MORRIS. It's late.

ZACHARIAH. I want to have a good look at you, man.

MORRIS. It's a bit late in the day to be seeing your brother for the first time. I been here a whole year, now, you know.

ZACHARIAH. Ja. But after a whole life I only seen me properly tonight. You helped me. I'm grateful.

MORRIS. It was nothing—

ZACHARIAH. No! I'm not a man that forgets a favour. I want to help you now.

MORRIS. I don't need any assistance, thank you.

ZACHARIAH. Sit down. (*MORRIS sits.*) You're on the lighter side of life all right. You like that . . . all over? Your legs and things?

MORRIS. It's evenly spread.

ZACHARIAH. Not even a foot in the darker side, hey! I'd say you must be quite a bright boy with nothing on.

MORRIS. Please, Zach!

ZACHARIAH. You're shy! Ja. You always get undressed in the dark. Always well closed up. Like Ethel. I bet she shines. You know something. I bet if it was you she saw and not me she wouldn't say nothing. (*MORRIS closes his eyes and gives a light, nervous laugh. ZACHARIAH also laughs, but hollowly.*) I'm sure she wouldn't be surprised, or laugh, or swear or scream. Nobody would come running. I bet she would just say: How do you do, Mr. Pietersen? (*pause*) There's a thought there, Morrie. You ever think of it?

MORRIS. No.

ZACHARIAH. Not even a little bit of it? Like there, where you say: "Hello, Ethel—" and shake her hand. You'd manage all right, Morrie. One thing is for certain: you would look all right, with her, and that's the main thing, hey?

MORRIS. You're dreaming again, Zach.

ZACHARIAH. No, man! This is not my sort of dream. (*He laughs.*) I didn't shake her hands. You're the man for shaking hands, Morrie.

MORRIS. Finished, Zach?

ZACHARIAH. No. We're still coming to the big thought. Why don't you meet her? (*pause*)

MORRIS. You want to know why?

ZACHARIAH. Ja.

MORRIS. You really want to know?

ZACHARIAH. I do.

MORRIS. She's not my pen-pal. (*MORRIS moves to get up. ZACHARIAH stops him.*)

ZACHARIAH. All right. Let's try it another way. Would you like to meet her?

MORRIS. Listen, Zach. I've told you before. Ethel is your —

ZACHARIAH. (*pained*) Please, Morrie! Would — you — like — to — meet — her?

MORRIS. That's no sort of question.

ZACHARIAH. Why not?

MORRIS. Because all my life I've been interested in meeting people. I'm telling you the question is meaningless.

ZACHARIAH. Okay, I'll put it this way. Would you like to see her, or hear her, or maybe touch her?

MORRIS. That still doesn't give the question any meaning! And anyway, Ethel is your pen-pal.

ZACHARIAH. Right. Wait! You can have her.

MORRIS. What's this now?

ZACHARIAH. She's yours. I'm giving her to you.

MORRIS. (*angry*) This is no game, Zach!

ZACHARIAH. But I mean it. Look. I can't use her. We seen that. She'll see it too. But why throw away a good pen-pal if somebody else can do it? You can. When Ethel sees you all she will say is: "How do you do, Mr. Pietersen?" She'll never know otherwise.

MORRIS. You think so?

ZACHARIAH. You could fool me, Morrie, if I didn't know who you was.

MORRIS. You mean that, Zach?

ZACHARIAH. Cross my heart and hope to die. And the way you can talk! She'd be impressed.

MORRIS. That's true. I like to talk.

ZACHARIAH. No harm in it, man. A couple of words, a little walk and a packet of monkey-nuts on the way.

MORRIS. Monkey-nuts?

ZACHARIAH. Tickey a packet. Something to chew.

MORRIS. Good God, Zach! You take a lady friend to tea, man!

ZACHARIAH. To tea, hey!

MORRIS. With buns, if she's hungry. Hot-cross buns.

ZACHARIAH. Now, you see! I would have just bought monkey-nuts. She's definitely not for me.

MORRIS. Yes, to tea. A pot of afternoon tea. When she sits down, you pull out the chair . . . like this. (*He demonstrates.*)

ZACHARIAH. I think I seen that.

MORRIS. The woman pours the tea but the man butters the bun.

ZACHARIAH. Well, well, well.

MORRIS. Only two spoons of sugar, and don't drink out of the saucer.

ZACHARIAH. Very good.

MORRIS. If she wants to blow her nose, offer your hanky, which you keep in a breast pocket.

ZACHARIAH. Go on.

MORRIS. (*waking up to reality*) It's no good! You're wasting my time. I'm going to bed.

ZACHARIAH. But what's the matter, man? You were telling me everything so damn good. Come on. Tell me. (*coaxing*) Tell your brother what's the matter.

MORRIS. I haven't got a hanky.

ZACHARIAH. I think we can buy one.

MORRIS. And the breast pocket?

ZACHARIAH. What's the problem there? Let's also—

MORRIS. Don't be a bloody fool! You got to buy a whole suit to get the breast pocket. And that's still not all. What about socks, decent shoes, a spotty tie and a clean white shirt? How do you think a man steps out to meet a waiting lady. On his bare feet, wearing rags, and stinking because he hasn't had a bath? She'd even laugh and scream at me if I went like this. So I'm giving Ethel back to you. There's nothing I can do with her, thank you very much. (*MORRIS crosses to his bed. ZACHARIAH thinks.*)

ZACHARIAH. Haven't we got enough money?

MORRIS. All I got left is one shilling, and until you get paid . . . What am I talking about! You know what a right sort of for-a-meeting-with-the-lady type of suit costs? Pounds and pounds and pounds. Shoes? Pounds and pounds. Shirt? Pounds. And then there's still two socks and a tie.

ZACHARIAH. (*patiently*) We got that sort of money.

MORRIS. Here it is. One shilling. Take it and go and buy me a suit, please.

ZACHARIAH. Thank you. (*takes the coin and throws it away without even looking at it*) Where's the tin?

MORRIS. Tin?

ZACHARIAH. Round sort of tin.

MORRIS. (*horror*) Our tin?

ZACHARIAH. There was sweets in it at Christmas.

MORRIS. You mean, our future?

ZACHARIAH. That's the one. The future tin.

MORRIS. Our two-man farm?

ZACHARIAH. Where is it?

MORRIS. I won't tell you. (*He runs and stands spread-eagled in front of the cupboard where the tin is hidden.*)

ZACHARIAH. Ah-ha!

MORRIS. No, Zach!

ZACHARIAH. Give it to me!

MORRIS. I won't! I won't! (*Grabs the tin and runs away. ZACHARIAH lurches after him. MORRIS is quick and elusive.*)

ZACHARIAH. I'll catch you, Morrie, and when I do—

MORRIS. Zach, please! Just stop! Please! Just stand still and listen to me. Everything . . . everything we got, the most precious thing a man can have, a future, is in here. You've worked hard, I've done the saving.

ZACHARIAH. We'll start again.

MORRIS. It will take too long.

ZACHARIAH. I'll work overtime.

MORRIS. It won't be the same. (*ZACHARIAH lunges suddenly, but MORRIS escapes.*)

ZACHARIAH. Bliksem! Wait, Morrie! Wait! Fair is fair. Now this time you stand still . . . and think. Ethel—

MORRIS. I won't

ZACHARIAH. Yes, you will, because Ethel is coming and you want to meet her. But like you say, not like any Hotnot in the street, but smartly. Now this is it. You're wearing a pretty-smart-for-a-meeting-with-the-lady type of suit. (*MORRIS, clutching the tin to his chest, closes his eyes. ZACHARIAH creeps closer.*) Shiny shoes, white socks, a good shirt and a spotty tie. And the people watch you go by and say: Hey! Hey! Just come and look, man. Will you please just come and look at that! . . . There goes something! And Ethel says: "Who's this coming? Could it be my friend, Mr. Pietersen?" And you say: "Good day to you, Miss Ethel. May I shake your white hands with my white hands?" "Of course, Mr. Pietersen." (*ZACHARIAH has reached MORRIS. He takes the tin.*) Thank you, Morrie. (*MORRIS doesn't move. ZACHARIAH opens the tin, takes out the money and then callously throws the tin away. He takes the money to the table where he counts it.*)

MORRIS. Why are you doing this to me?

ZACHARIAH. Aren't we brothers? (*pause*)

MORRIS. Where was I? Yes. At a garage, on the floor, with Kleinbooi and there were moths. Then I had that deep thought. You see they were flying in out of the darkness . . . to the lamp . . . into the flame. Always to light, I thought. Everything always flying, or growing, or turning, or crying for the whiteness of light. Birds following the sun when winter comes; trees and things standing, begging for it; moths hunting it; Man watching it. All of us, always, out of darkness and into light.

ZACHARIAH. What sort of suit? And what about the shoes?

MORRIS. Go to a good shop. Ask for the outfit, for a gentleman.

ACT THREE

Scene 1

The next day. MORRIS is lying on his bed, staring up at the ceiling. There is a knock at the door. MORRIS rises slowly on his bed.

MORRIS. Who is there? (*The knock is heard again.*) Speak up. I can't hear. (*Silence. MORRIS's fear is now apparent. He waits until the knock is heard a third time.*) Ethel . . . I mean, Madam . . . no, no! . . . I mean to say, Miss Ethel Lange, could that be you? (*In reply there is a raucous burst of laughter, unmistakably ZACHARIAH's.*) What's this? (*silence*) What's the meaning of this? (*MORRIS rushes to his bed and looks at the alarm clock.*) Zach! It's still only the middle of the day. Go back to work! At once!

ZACHARIAH. I can't.

MORRIS. Why not?

ZACHARIAH. I took some leave, Morris, and left. Let me in.

MORRIS. What's the matter with you? The door's not locked.

ZACHARIAH. My hands are full. (*pause*) I been shopping, Morrie. (*MORRIS rushes to the door, but collects himself before opening it. ZACHARIAH comes in, his arms piled high with parcels. He smiles slyly at MORRIS, who has assumed a pose of indifference.*) So you thought it was maybe our little Miss Ethel. Well, don't worry no more, Morrie, because you know what these is? Your outfit! Number one, and what do we have? A wonderful hat . . . sir. (*Takes it out and holds it up for approval. His manner is exaggerated and suggestive of*

59

the shopkeeper who sold him the clothing.) Guaranteed to protect the head on Sundays and rainy days. Number two is the shirt, and a grey tie, which is much better taste. Spots are too loud for a gentleman. Next we have — two grey socks, left and right, and a hanky to blow her nose. (*next parcel*) Aha! We've come to the suit. Now before I show you the suit, my friend, I want to ask you, what does a man really look for in a good suit? A good cloth. Isn't that so?

MORRIS. What are you talking about?

ZACHARIAH. That's what he said. The fashion might be a season old, but will you please feel the difference. It's lasted for years already. All I can say is, take it or leave it. But remember, only a fool would leave it at that price. So I took it. (*next parcel*) Here we have a real Ostrich wallet.

MORRIS. What for?

ZACHARIAH. Your inside pocket. Ja! You forgot about the inside pocket. A gentleman always got a wallet for the inside pocket. (*next parcel*) And a cigarette lighter, and a cigarette case. Chramonium!

MORRIS. Since when do I smoke?

ZACHARIAH. Ethel might, he said.

MORRIS. (*fear*) You told him?

ZACHARIAH. Don't worry. I just said there was a lady who someone was going to meet. He winked at me and said it was a good thing, now and then, and reminded me that ladies like presents. (*holds up a scarf*) A pretty doek in case the wind blows her hair away, he said. Here we got an umbrella in case it's sopping wet. And over here . . . (*last parcel*) Guess! Come on, Morrie. Guess what's in this box. I'll shake it. Listen.

MORRIS. Shoes.

ZACHARIAH. (*triumphantly*) No! It's boots! I got you

boots. Ha, ha! Ja. (*watching MORRIS's reaction*) They frighten a ou, don't they? (*happy*) Satisfied?

MORRIS. (*looking at the pile of clothing*) It seems all right.

ZACHARIAH. It wasn't easy. At the first shop, when I asked for the outfit for a gentleman, they said I was an agitator and was going to call the police. I had to get out, man . . . quick! Even this fellow . . . Mr. Moses . . . "Come again my friend. You're drunk," he said. But when I showed him our future he sobered up. You know what he said? "Are you the gentleman?" So I said: "Do I look like a gentleman, Mr. Moses?" He said: "My world." "I'm the black sort," I said. So he said: "You don't say." Go ahead, Morrie. (*the clothing*) Let's see the gentle sort of man.

MORRIS. Okay. Okay. Don't rush me. (*Moves cautiously to the pile of clothing. Flicks an imaginary speck of dust off the hat. ZACHARIAH is waiting.*) Well? (*ZACHARIAH is waiting.*) Give me time.

ZACHARIAH. What for?

MORRIS. For God's sake, Zach! This is deep water. I'm not just going to jump right in. You must paddle around first.

ZACHARIAH. Paddle around? (*offering him the hat*) Try it on.

MORRIS. The idea, man. I got to try it on. There's more to wearing a white skin than just putting on a hat. You've seen white men before without hats, but they're still white men, aren't they?

ZACHARIAH. Ja.

MORRIS. And without suits or socks, or shoes . . .

ZACHARIAH. No, Morrie. Never without socks and shoes. Never a barefoot white man.

MORRIS. Well, the suit then. Look, Zach, what I'm

trying to say is this. The clothes will help, but only help. They don't maketh the white man. It's that white something inside you, that special meaning and manner of whiteness that I got to find. I know what I'm talking about because . . . I'll be honest with you now, Zach. . . . I've thought about it for a long time. What do you think I'm thinking about when I'm not saying something? I'm being critical of colour, and the first fruit of my thought is that this whiteness of theirs is not just in the skin, otherwise . . . well, I mean . . . I'd be one of them, wouldn't I? Because, let me tell you, I seen them that's darker than me. Yes. Really dark, man. Only they had that something I'm telling you about . . . and, let me tell you, it's even in their way of walking.

ZACHARIAH. So you must learn to walk properly then.

MORRIS. Yes.

ZACHARIAH. And to look right at things.

MORRIS. Yes.

ZACHARIAH. And to sound right.

MORRIS. Yes! There's that, as well. The sound of it.

ZACHARIAH. So go on. (*again offering the hat*) Try it. For size. Just for the sake of the size. (*MORRIS takes the hat, plays with it for a few seconds, then impulsively puts it on.*) Ha!

MORRIS. Yes?

ZACHARIAH. Aha!

MORRIS. (*whipping off the hat in embarrassment*) No.

ZACHARIAH. Yes.

MORRIS. (*shaking his head*) Uhuh!

ZACHARIAH. Come.

MORRIS. No, man.

ZACHARIAH. Please, man.

MORRIS. You're teasing.

ZACHARIAH. No, man. I like the look of that on your head.

MORRIS. Really?

ZACHARIAH. S'true's God.

MORRIS. It looked right?

ZACHARIAH. I'm telling you.

MORRIS. It seemed to fit.

ZACHARIAH. It did, I know.

MORRIS. (*using this as an excuse to get it back on his head*) The brim was just right on the brow . . . and with plenty of room for the brain! I'll try it again, shall I? (*lifting the hat*) Good morning!

ZACHARIAH. Very good.

MORRIS. Did it look right? (*again*) Good morning . . . Miss Ethel Lange! (*Looks quickly to see ZACHARIAH's reaction. He betrays nothing.*)

ZACHARIAH. Maybe a little bit higher.

MORRIS. (*again*) Good morning . . . (*a flourish*) and how do you do today, Miss Ethel Lange! (*laughing with delight*) How about the jacket?

ZACHARIAH. Okay. (*Hands him the jacket. MORRIS puts it on.*)

MORRIS. (*preening*) How did you do it?

ZACHARIAH. I said: The gentleman is smaller than me, Mr. Moses.

MORRIS. It's so smug. Look, Zach, I'm going to do that little bit again. Watch me careful. (*once again lifting his hat*) Good day, Miss Ethel Lange . . . (*pleading, servile*) I beg your pardon, but I do hope you wouldn't mind to take a little walk with . . .

ZACHARIAH. Stop!

MORRIS. What's wrong?

ZACHARIAH. Your voice.

MORRIS. What's wrong with it?

ZACHARIAH. Too soft. They don't never sound like that.

MORRIS. To a lady they do! I admit, if it wasn't Ethel I was addressing it would be different.

ZACHARIAH. Okay. Try me.

MORRIS. How?

ZACHARIAH. You're walking with Ethel. I'm selling monkey-nuts.

MORRIS. So?

ZACHARIAH. So you want some monkey-nuts.

MORRIS. That's a good idea . . . (*His voice trails off.*)

ZACHARIAH. Go on. I'm selling monkey-nuts. Monkey-nuts. Monkey-nuts.

MORRIS. (*after hesitation*) I can't.

ZACHARIAH. (*simulated shock*) What!

MORRIS. (*frightened*) What I mean is . . . I don't want any monkey-nuts. I'm not hungry.

ZACHARIAH. Ethel wants some. And I'm selling them.

MORRIS. This is hard for me, Zach.

ZACHARIAH. You must learn your lesson, Morrie. You want to pass, don't you? Monkey-nuts.

MORRIS. (*steeling himself*) Excuse me!

ZACHARIAH. I'll never hear that.

MORRIS. Hey!

ZACHARIAH. Or that.

MORRIS. Boy!

ZACHARIAH. I'm ignoring you, man. I'm a cheeky one.

MORRIS. You're asking for it, Zach!

ZACHARIAH. I am. Go ahead.

MORRIS. (*with brutality and coarseness*) Hey, Swart-gat! (*An immediate reaction from ZACHARIAH. His head whips around. He stares at MORRIS in disbelief. MORRIS replies with a weak little laugh, which soon*

dies on his lips.) Just a joke! (*softly*) Forgive me, Zach.
Don't look at me like that! (*A step to ZACHARIAH,
who backs away.*) Say something. For God's sake, say
anything! I'm your brother.

ZACHARIAH. (*disbelief*) My brother?

MORRIS. Me, Zach, Morris!

ZACHARIAH. Morris?

MORRIS. (*He at last realises what has happened. He
tears off the jacket and hat in a frenzy.*) Now do you
see?

ZACHARIAH. It's you. That's funny. I thought . . . I
was looking, I thought, at a different sort of man.

MORRIS. But don't you see, Zach? It was me! That
different sort of man you saw was me. And I swear, I no
longer wanted it. That's why I came back. Because . . .
because . . . I'll tell you the whole truth now . . .
Because I did try it! It didn't seem a sin. If a man was
born with a chance at change, why not take it? I
thought . . . thinking of worms lying warm in their silk,
to come out one day with wings and things! Why not a
man? If his dreams are soft and keep him warm at
night, why not stand up the next morning.
Different . . . Beautiful! So . . . so . . . so what was
worrying me? You. What sort of thing was that to do to
a ou's own flesh and blood brother? Anywhere,
anyplace or road, there was you. So I came back.
(*Pause. The alarm rings. Neither responds.*)

SCENE 2

*Night. The two men are asleep. Silence. Suddenly
ZACHARIAH sits up in bed. Without looking at
MORRIS he gets up, goes to the corner where the*

*new suit of clothes is hanging, and puts on the suit
and hat. The final effect is an absurdity bordering
on the grotesque. The hat is too small and so is the
jacket, which he has buttoned up incorrectly, while
the trousers are too short. ZACHARIAH stands
barefooted, holding the umbrella, the hat pulled
down low over his eyes so that his face is almost
hidden.*

ZACHARIAH. Ma. Ma! Mother! Hullo. How are you,
old woman? What's that? You don't recognise me?
Well, well, well. Take a guess. (*shakes his head*) What's
the matter with you, Ma? Don't you recognise your own
son? (*shakes his head violently*) No, no! Not him! It's
me, Zach! (*sweeps off the hat to show his face*) Ja.
Zach! Didn't think I could do it, did you? Well, to tell
you the truth, the whole truth so help me God, I got sick
of myself and made a change. Him? At home, Ma. Ja.
A lonely boy, as you say. He went on the road, Ma, but
strange to say, he came back quite white. No tan at all. I
don't recognise him no more. (*He sits.*) I'll ask you
again, how are you, old woman? I see some signs of
wear and tear. (*nodding his head*) That's true . . . such
sorrow . . . Ja . . . it's cruel . . . and your feet as well?
Still a bad fit in the shoe? Ai ai ai? Me? (*Pause. He
struggles.*) There's something I need to know, Ma. You
see, we been talking, me and him . . . ja, I talk to him,
he says it helps . . . and and now we got to know.
Whose mother were you really? At the bottom of your
heart, tell me, whom did you really love? No evil feelings, Ma, but, I mean a man's got to know. You see,
he's been such a burden as a brother. (*agitation*) Don't
be dumb. Don't cry! It was just a question! Look! I
brought you a present, old soul. (*holds out a hand with*

the fingers lightly closed) It's a butterfly. A real beauty butterfly. We were traveling fast, Ma. We hit them at ninety . . . a whole flock. But one was still alive, and it made me think of . . . Mother . . . So I caught it, myself, for you, remembering what I caught from you. This, old Ma of mine, is gratitude for you, and it proves it, doesn't it? Some things are only skin deep, because I got it, here in my hand, I got beauty . . . too . . . haven't I?

SCENE 3

The next evening. For the first time the room is untidy. The beds are not made, the table is cluttered, the floor littered with the strings and wrappings of the parcels of the previous day. MORRIS is alone. He sits lifelessly at the table, his head fallen on his chest, his arms hanging limp at his sides. On the table is a small bundle. Then ZACHARIAH comes in. He behaves normally, going straight to the bed and taking off his shoes. Only when this is done, does he realise something is wrong. The footbath hasn't been prepared.

ZACHARIAH. What's this? (*looking around for the basin*) Footsalts finished? Hell, man! Couldn't you have seen? What must I do now? My feet are killing me again. I've been on them today, you know. (*touching the toes*) Eina! Eina! Forget the salts then. Just give me some hot. A soak will do them good. (*MORRIS doesn't move.*) Some hot, Morrie! Please! (*Nothing happens.*) What's the matter with you? Don't tell me the stove is buggered up! (*goes to the stove and feels the kettle*) Ag, no, man! What the hell's happened? A man works all day, his feet are killing him and he comes home and finds this (*the stove*) . . . and this. (*the room*) Floor not swept! Beds not made! (*Beginning to realise. MORRIS struggles to find a word, but fails and drops his shoulders in a gesture of defeat and resignation. Disbelief.*) . . . You mean you got nothing to say? (*A little laugh, but this quickly dies. Desperate.*) What happened?

MORRIS. I've given up.

ZACHARIAH. What?

MORRIS. I mean, I can't carry on.

ZACHARIAH. Oh, so you've just stopped.

MORRIS. Yes.

ZACHARIAH. But that won't do! Emphatically not! A man can't stop just like that, like you. That's definitely no good, because . . . Because a man must carry on. (*sees the bundle on the table for the first time*) What's this bundle, Morrie?

MORRIS. My belongings.

ZACHARIAH. What's that?

MORRIS. My Bible, my other shirt and my alarm clock.

ZACHARIAH. What for?

MORRIS. I was leaving, Zach.

ZACHARIAH. Leaving?

MORRIS. Going away.

ZACHARIAH. Where?

MORRIS. The road. Wherever it went.

ZACHARIAH. Oh! (*pause*) And what about me?

MORRIS. I know, I know.

ZACHARIAH. But you don't care, hey?

MORRIS. I do care, Zach!

ZACHARIAH. (*ignoring the denial*) That's a fine thought for a loving brother.

MORRIS. Stop it, Zach! I'm still here. I wrapped up my Bible and my clock in my shirt and wrote the farewell note. (*pause*)

ZACHARIAH. Come on, cheer up. It's not so bad.

MORRIS. I can't, Zach. Honestly I can't anymore. I know I can't go . . . but I've given up.

ZACHARIAH. But I've got a surprise for you.

MORRIS. It will have to be damn good to make any difference.

ZACHARIAH. How good is a letter from Ethel?

MORRIS. No damn good! You've missed the point. Don't you see, man! She's to blame. (*ZACHARIAH takes out the letter.*) I don't want it. Take it away.

ZACHARIAH. (*putting the letter down on the table so that MORRIS can see it*) It's not mine. I gave her to you.

MORRIS. Everything was fine until she came along.

ZACHARIAH. She hasn't yet.

MORRIS. What do you mean?

ZACHARIAH. Come along. You've missed the problem. Ethel coming along was the problem. She hasn't yet. But she might be on her way. I mean . . . It could be June, couldn't it? And one fine day, you know what? Guess.

MORRIS. What?

ZACHARIAH. Another knock at the door. But it won't be me. So, you see, if I was you, just for safety's sake, of course, I'd have a quick peep at that letter. (*ZACHARIAH goes to his bed. MORRIS hesitates for a second, then takes the letter, opens it and reads in silence. When he has finished he puts it down and looks at ZACHARIAH vacantly. ZACHARIAH is unable to contain himself any longer.*) She's coming! Let me guess. She's on the train, on her way, and it's June. When do you meet, man? What did she say? Tell me, Morrie.

MORRIS. No. She's not coming. Never. Prepare yourself for . . . good news. Ethel's gone and got engaged to get married, to Luckyman Stoffel.

ZACHARIAH. No.

MORRIS. Yes.

ZACHARIAH. No.

MORRIS. S'true's God.

ZACHARIAH. No!

MORRIS. Then listen. (*reads*) "Dear Pen-pal, it's sad news for you but good news for me. I've decided to get married. Ma says it's okay. The lucky man is Stoffel, who plays in my brother's team, fullback. It's a long story. Lucy thought she had him, but she didn't, so now we're not on talking terms no more. Stoffel works at Boetie's Garage and doesn't like competition so he says pen-pals is out if we're going to get married to each other. He's sitting here now and he says he wants to say this: 'Leave my woman alone if you know what's good for you.' That was Stoffel. He's a one all right. Well, pal, that's all for now, for ever. Ethel." (*pause*) Down here at the bottom she says: "You can keep the snapshot for a keepsake." (*MORRIS looks vacantly at ZACHARIAH whose attitude has hardened with bitter disappointment.*)

ZACHARIAH. So?

MORRIS. So I think we can begin again.

ZACHARIAH. What?

MORRIS. That's a good question. (*pause*) Well, let's work it out. Where are we? Here. That's a good beginning. What is this? Our house. Me and you, Morrie and Zach . . . live here . . . in peace because the problem's gone . . . and got engaged to be married . . . and I'm Morrie . . . and I was going to go, but now I'm going to stay! (*With something of his old self, MORRIS goes to work, opens his bundle and packs out his belongings.*) Hey, Zach! (*holding up the clock*) It's stopped. Like me. What time shall we make it? Supper!

ZACHARIAH. I'm not hungry.

MORRIS. Bedtime?

ZACHARIAH. I don't want to sleep.

MORRIS. Just after supper, then. We'll say we've eaten.

ZACHARIAH. You can say what you like!

MORRIS. What's the matter? Come on, now. Tell me what it is.

ZACHARIAH. (*slowly*) You aren't going to wear that suit anymore?

MORRIS. I see. Zach, look at me now. Solemnly, on this Bible, I promise you I won't.

ZACHARIAH. (*slyly*) You looked so damn smart in that suit, Morrie. It made me feel good.

MORRIS. You mean that?

ZACHARIAH. Cross my heart.

MORRIS. You mean you want to see me *in it*?

ZACHARIAH. I do.

MORRIS. Be honest now, Zach. Is what you are saying that you would like me to put that suit on?

ZACHARIAH. (*emphatically*) Now.

MORRIS. Now! This comes as a surprise, Zach. But if as you say it makes you feel better . . . well . . . that just about makes it my duty, doesn't it? (*moving to the suit*) It was a damn good buy, Ethel or no Ethel.

ZACHARIAH. Then get in.

MORRIS. You'll have to help me. It's not so easy now . . . after yesterday. Say something to help me.

ZACHARIAH. Just for size. No harm done. We're brothers. She's gone for good. Nothing to worry about. This is just between us. We're only playing now.

MORRIS. Only playing! Of course! That does it. (*With a laugh MORRIS puts on the suit. When he is dressed, he walks around the room in exaggerated style. ZACHARIAH encourages him.*)

ZACHARIAH. Ek se! Just look! Hoe's dit vir 'n ding. Links draai, regs swaai . . . Aitsa! Ou pellie, you're stepping high tonight!

MORRIS. (*He stops, turns suddenly.*) Hey Swartgat! (*A second of silence, and then ZACHARIAH laughs.*) No harm done now, hey, Zach?

ZACHARIAH. No pain.

MORRIS. That's the way to take a joke. (*again*) Hey, Swartgat!

ZACHARIAH. (*playing along*) Ja, Baas?

MORRIS. Who are you?

ZACHARIAH. I'm your boy, Zach, Baas.

MORRIS. Who am I?

ZACHARIAH. Baas Morrie, Baas.

MORRIS. Baas Morrie and his boy, Zach! My god, you're comical! Where the hell you get that joke from, Zach?

ZACHARIAH. At the gate.

MORRIS. So that's what it's like.

ZACHARIAH. They're all dressed up smart like you, and go walking by. Go on. Try it.

MORRIS. What?

ZACHARIAH. Walk past.

MORRIS. You want to play it?

ZACHARIAH. Why not?

MORRIS. I haven't seen the gate before, Zach. It's difficult to play something you haven't seen.

ZACHARIAH. I'll show you. Here it is. (*vague gesture*) This here is the gate.

MORRIS. What's on the other side?

ZACHARIAH. Does it matter?

MORRIS. It does if we're going to play this thing right.

ZACHARIAH. (*looking back*) Trees.

MORRIS. Ah. Tall trees, with picnics in the shade.

ZACHARIAH. Grass.

MORRIS. Green, hey! We'll make it spring.

ZACHARIAH. Flowers with butterflies.

MORRIS. That's a good touch.

ZACHARIAH. And benches.

MORRIS. How thoughtful! I'll want to rest.

ZACHARIAH. And I'm squatting here.

MORRIS. Right. So you'll open the gate for me when I get there.

ZACHARIAH. No. It's open. I'll just watch your boots as you go by.

MORRIS. Then what's your job at the gate?

ZACHARIAH. (*pause*) They put me there to chase the black kids away. (*MORRIS hesitates.*)

MORRIS. Are you sure we should play this?

ZACHARIAH. It's only a game. Walk past.

MORRIS. (*He flourishes his umbrella and then saunters slowly towards ZACHARIAH.*) Shame! Look at that poor old boy. John? What are you doing . . . ?

ZACHARIAH. (*cutting him*) No, Morrie.

MORRIS. What's wrong?

ZACHARIAH. They never talk to me. Start again. (*MORRIS tries it again. This time he doesn't speak, but pretends to take a coin out of his pocket and tosses it to ZACHARIAH.*) How much?

MORRIS. Half a crown.

ZACHARIAH. What!

MORRIS. Shilling.

ZACHARIAH. Too much.

MORRIS. Sixpence. (*ZACHARIAH is still doubtful.*) All right then, a penny.

ZACHARIAH. That's a bit better, but—

MORRIS. But what?

ZACHARIAH. You think you're the soft sort of white man, hey! Giving me a penny like that.

MORRIS. What's wrong with being the soft sort? You find them.

ZACHARIAH. I know. But not you. Not with boots, Morrie. Never with boots. That sort doesn't even see me. So don't stop. Just walk past.

MORRIS. (*The mime is repeated. This time MORRIS walks straight past.*) Now what?

ZACHARIAH. I have a thought. I'm squatting here, watching you, and I think.

MORRIS. Okay.

ZACHARIAH. Bastard!

MORRIS. (*sharply*) Who?

ZACHARIAH. Don't spoil it, man! You don't hear me. It's a thought. (*taps his forehead*)

MORRIS. (*looking away, frowning*) Carry on. What happens now?

ZACHARIAH. I'm watching you, but you're looking up at the trees, remember?

MORRIS. Yes, of course. It's a tall tree. I'm wondering if I've ever seen a tree as tall as this tree. There's also a great weight of birdies on the branches and . . . actually I'm finding difficulty keeping my mind up the tree with you behind my back. I feel your presence. So I think, I'll move further on . . . I'll have to get away if I want to admire the beauty, won't I? Yes. It's a good road. It's going places, because ahead of me I see the sky. I see it through the trees . . . so I'm climbing up the hill in this road, putting miles between us; and now, at last, there ahead of me is the sky, big, blue; and I hurry on to the top where I turn against it and look back at you . . . far behind me now, in the distance, outside the gate. Can you see me?

ZACHARIAH. A little.

MORRIS. What is it you see here, in the distance, beyond the trees, upon the hill, against the sky?

ZACHARIAH. Could it be a . . . man?

MORRIS. A white man! Don't you see the way I stand? What do you think now?

ZACHARIAH. He's a bastard!

MORRIS. (*reckless in his elation*) Well, I don't care. In fact, I'm almost free . . . I can run now! I go, laughing, over the green spring grass, into the flowers and among the butterflies. And what do I say? What do I shout? I've changed! Look at me, will you please! (*pause*) Now I'm tired. After so many years, so much beauty is a burden. I need rest. (*sits*) Ah, dearie, dearie me. (*ZACHARIAH comes past, bent low, miming the picking up of litter in the park. One hand trails a sack, the other is stabbing with a stick at pieces of paper. MORRIS watches this with critical interest.*) What are you doing?

ZACHARIAH. Picking up rubbish. I got a stick with a nail on the end. Every afternoon, at four o'clock, I go through the trees and around the benches and pick up the papers and peels.

MORRIS. I thought I left you behind.

ZACHARIAH. I know.

MORRIS. The sight of you affects me, Swartgat.

ZACHARIAH. (*continuing with his mime*) I can feel it does.

MORRIS. It's interesting. Just looking at you does it. I don't need the other senses. Just the sight of you crawling around like some . . . thing . . . makes me want to bring it up.

ZACHARIAH. Is that so?

MORRIS. (*rising*) In fact I'd like to . . . (*stops himself*)

ZACHARIAH. Carry on.

MORRIS. (*walking away*) I can't.

ZACHARIAH. Try.

MORRIS. I'm telling you I can't.

ZACHARIAH. Why?

MORRIS. Not with that old woman watching us. (*ZACHARIAH stops and looks questioningly at MORRIS.*) Over there. (*pointing*)

ZACHARIAH. Old woman?

MORRIS. Horribly old.

ZACHARIAH. Alone?

MORRIS. All by her lonely self.

ZACHARIAH. And she's watching us?

MORRIS. All the time. (*impatience*) Can't you *see!* She's wearing a grey dress on Sunday.

ZACHARIAH. (*recognition dawning*) Soapsuds . . .

MORRIS. . . . on brown hands.

ZACHARIAH. And sore feet! The toes are crooked, hey!

MORRIS. She's been following me all day . . . begging!

ZACHARIAH. Call the police.

MORRIS. No, no. Not that.

ZACHARIAH. Then what will we do?

MORRIS. Let's work it out. We can't carry on with her watching us . . . behind that bush . . . like an old spy.

ZACHARIAH. So she must go.

MORRIS. I think so, too. (*a step in the direction of the old woman*) Go away.

ZACHARIAH. Is she moving?

MORRIS. No. (*trying again*) Go away, old one! Begat and be gone! Go home! (*sigh*) It's no use.

ZACHARIAH. (*trying to scare her off*) Hey!

MORRIS. (*excited*) She jumped! Ha ha. She jumped!

ZACHARIAH. Voertsek!

MORRIS. Another jump. (*ZACHARIAH goes down on his hands and knees.*) What are you doing?

ZACHARIAH. Stones.

MORRIS. Hooooooo! She heard you. She's trotted off a little distance. But you're not really going to use them, are you?

ZACHARIAH. It's the only way. (*throws*)

MORRIS. Almost. (*ZACHARIAH throws again.*) She jumped!

ZACHARIAH. Voertsek!

MORRIS. Yes. Voertsek off! We don't want you!

ZACHARIAH. Bugger off!

MORRIS. You old bitch! You made life unbearable!

ZACHARIAH. (*starts throwing with renewed violence*) Hamba!

MORRIS. She's running now.

ZACHARIAH. Get out!

MORRIS. Kaffermeid!

ZACHARIAH. Ou hoer!

MORRIS. Luisgat!

ZACHARIAH. Swartgat!

MORRIS. You've hit her! She's down. Look . . . Look!

ZACHARIAH. Look at those old legs sticking up!

MORRIS. She's got no pants on! (*Their derision rises to a climax, MORRIS shaking his umbrella, ZACHARIAH his fists.*) That's the last of her I think.

By God, she ran! (*Pause while they get their breath.*) Where were we?

ZACHARIAH. It was four o'clock. I was collecting the rubbish. You wanted to do . . . something.

MORRIS. Yes. I remember now. I just wanted to . . . just wanted to . . . Poke you with my umbrella. He-he-he! (*He attacks ZACHARIAH savagely.*) Just wanted to poke you a little bit. That's all. He-he! What do you think umbrellas are for when it doesn't rain? Hey? (*ZACHARIAH tries to escape, but MORRIS catches him with the crook of the umbrella.*) Wait, wait! Not so fast, John. I want to have a good look at you. My God! What sort of mistake is this? A black man? All over, my boy?

ZACHARIAH. Ja, Baas.

MORRIS. Your pits and privates?

ZACHARIAH. Ja, Baas.

MORRIS. Nothing white?

ZACHARIAH. Forgive me please, my Baas.

MORRIS. You're horrible.

ZACHARIAH. Sorry, Baas.

MORRIS. You stink.

ZACHARIAH. Please, my Baasie . . .

MORRIS. You don't use paper, do you?

ZACHARIAH. . . . . oh, my Baasie, my Baasie, my good little Baasie.

MORRIS. What did you mean crawling around like that? Spoiling the view, spoiling my chances! What's your game, hey? Trying to be an embarrassment? Is that it? A two-legged embarrassment? Well, I hate you, do you hear? Hate! . . . Hate! . . . Hate! . . . (*He attacks ZACHARIAH savagely with the umbrella. When his fury is spent he turns away and sits down.*) It was a good day. The sun shone. The sky was blue. I was happy. (*smiling, released of all tensions*) Not the sort of day to forget in a hurry. There's a spiny chill sprung up now, though. (*Shivering, ZACHARIAH is moaning softly.*) Something sighing among the trees . . . must be the wind. Yes! There were the trees as well today. The tall trees. So much to remember! Still . . . (*shivering*) . . . it has got nippy . . . and I haven't got an overcoat . . . with me.

ZACHARIAH. Ding-dong . . . ong . . . ong . . . Ding-dong . . . ong . . . ong.

MORRIS. What is that sound I hear?

ZACHARIAH. The bells. They're closing up. Ding-dong . . . ong . . . ong.

MORRIS. I'd better hurry home. (*stands*) Yes, it was a good day . . . while it lasted.

ZACHARIAH. Ding-dong . . . ong . . . ong.

MORRIS. Ah, there's the gate.

ZACHARIAH. What's the matter with you?

MORRIS. What's the matter with me?

ZACHARIAH. Can't you see the gate is locked?

MORRIS. Is it? (*tries the gate*) It is.

ZACHARIAH. I locked it before I rang the bell.

MORRIS. Heavens above! Then I'd better climb over.

ZACHARIAH. Over those sharp pieces of glass they got on the top?

MORRIS. Then the fence.

ZACHARIAH. Barbed wire . . . very high . . .

MORRIS. So what do I do?

ZACHARIAH. You might try calling.

MORRIS. Hello! Hello there! Hello, anybody there!

ZACHARIAH. Nobody hears you, hey!

MORRIS. Now what?

ZACHARIAH. Now you think you'll try the gate on the other side.

Morris. (*alarm*) All the way back?

Zachariah. Ja. (*moves quietly to the lamp on the table*)

Morris. Through the trees?

Zachariah. Looks like it.

Morris. But it's getting dark!

Zachariah. It happens every day.

Morris. And cold . . . and I never did like shadows . . . and . . . (*pause*) Where are you?

Zachariah. Behind a tree.

Morris. But . . . but I thought you were the good sort of boy?

Zachariah. Me?

Morris. The simple, trustworthy type of Johnboy. Weren't you that?

Zachariah. I've changed.

Morris. Who gave you the right?

Zachariah. I took it!

Morris. That's illegal! They weren't yours. That's theft. "Thou shalt not steal." I arrest you in the name of God. That's it! God! (*looking around wildly*) My prayers . . . (*MORRIS goes down on his knees. ZACHARIAH begins to move to him.*) Our Father, which art our Father in heaven, because we never knew the other one; forgive us this day our trespassing; I couldn't help it. The gate was open, God, so I didn't see the notice prohibiting! And "beware of the dog" was in Bantu, so how was I to know, Oh, Lord! My sins are not that black. Furthermore, just some bread for the poor, daily, and let Your Kingdom come as quick as it can, for Yours is the power and the glory, but ours is the fear and the judgment of eyes behind our back for the sins of our birth and the man behind the tree in the darkness while I wait . . . Eina! (*ZACHARIAH stands*

*above MORRIS on the point of violence. The alarm
clock rings. MORRIS crawls frantically away.*) Bed-
time! (*MORRIS jumps up, rushes to the table and turns
up the lamp. ZACHARIAH goes to his bed and sits. A
long silence. They avoid each other's eyes. MORRIS
takes off the jacket. At the window:*) Wind's turning
again. It's the mystery of my life, that lake. I mean . . .
It smells dead. doesn't it? If ever there was a piece of
water that looks dead and done for, that's what I'm
looking at now. (*leaving the window*) We'll sleep well
tonight, you'll see.

ZACHARIAH. Morris?

MORRIS. Yes?

ZACHARIAH. What happened?

MORRIS. We were carried away, as they would say, by
the game . . . Mustn't get worried, though . . . I'm sure
it's a good thing we got the game. It will pass the time.
Because we got a lot left, you know! (*little laugh*) . . .
Stretching ahead . . . in here . . . (*pause*) Yes.
(*pause*) . . . I'm not too worried. I mean, other men get
by without a future. In fact, I think there's quite a lot
of people getting by without futures these days. (*Silence.
MORRIS makes the last preparations for bed.*)

ZACHARIAH. Morris?

MORRIS. Yes?

ZACHARIAH. What is it, Morrie? The two of us . . .
you know . . . in here?

MORRIS. Home.

ZACHARIAH. Is there no other way?

MORRIS. No. You see, we're tied together, Zach. It's
what they call the blood knot . . . the bond between
brothers. (*As MORRIS moves to his bed:*)

CURTAIN

Other Publications for Your Interest

A LESSON FROM ALOES
(LITTLE THEATRE—DRAMA)

By ATHOL FUGARD

2 men, 1 woman—Interior

N.Y. Drama Critics Circle Award, Best Play of the Year. Set in a house in a white district of Port Elizabeth, South Africa, in 1963 this important new work by a truly major dramatist gives a compelling portrait of a society caught in the grip of a police state, and the effect it has on individuals. We are in the house of a liberal Afrikaner and his wife. He has been actively involved in anti-apartheid activity; she is recovering from a recent nervous breakdown brought about by a police raid on their home. They are waiting for a Black family to come to dinner (in South Africa, this is an absolutely forbidden act of insurrection). The Black family never arrives; but the head of the family does. He has just been released from prison and plans to flee South Africa—after first confronting the Afrikaner with the charge that he has betrayed him. "Exile, madness, utter loneliness—these are the only alternatives Mr. Fugard's characters have. What makes 'Aloes' so moving is the playwright's insistence on the heroism and integrity of these harsh choices."—N.Y. Times. "Immensely moving."—N.Y. Post. "One of the few dramatists in the world whose work really matters."—Newsweek. (#14146)

(Royalty, $60-$40, where available.)

MEETINGS
(BLACK GROUPS—COMEDY)

By MUSTAPHA MATURA

1 man, 2 women—Interiors

Greatly-acclaimed in its recent Off-Broadway production at New York's excellent Phoenix Theatre, *Meetings* is set in an ultra-modern kitchen which would be the dream of any American family—but it is in fast-developing Trinidad and is well-stocked with everything but food, much to the consternation of the husband, a successful engineer. His wife, an equally successful marketing executive, spends too much time at "meetings" (so does he)—and neither has time to actually *use* their kitchen. While the husband pines for some good down-home cooking, the wife is off pushing a new brand of cigarette ("Trini" is being used as a test-market). Soon, the local people are coughing up blood, and many die—apparently from the effects of smoking the new cigarette. Eventually, the husband goes "back to nature" and the wife succumbs to her own product. "An amazing piece of theatre . . . a highly literal parable about the poisoning of the tropical isle by modern commercialism."—Women's Wear Daily. "A bright, sharp comedy that turns into a sombre fable before our eyes."—The New Yorker. (#15659)

(Royalty, $50-$35.)

Other Publications for Your Interest

SPELL #7
(BLACK THEATRE GROUPS—CHOREOPOEM)

By NTOZAKE SHANGE, music by BUTCH MORRIS and DAVID MURRAY

4 men, 5 women—Interior

Another striking "choreopoem" from the pen of the author of *For Colored Girls . . .*! This one is set in St. Louis, in a bar frequented by Black artists and musicians, and is yet another meditation on the irony of being Black in a White world. Shange has her artists bare their souls in soliloquies, many of them illustrated by in-the-mood dances. "Spell #7 is humanely upbeat. In the end, (it) proclaims inner self-respect as the essential quality of black pride and black identity."—Christian Science Monitor. "An extremely fine theatre piece."—N.Y. Daily News. "A most lovely and powerful work."—N.Y. Times.

(Royalty, $50-$35.)

FOR COLORED GIRLS WHO HAVE CONSIDERED SUICIDE/WHEN THE RAINBOW IS ENUF
(LITTLE THEATRE)

By NTOZAKE SHANGE

7 women—Bare stage

For Colored Girls . . . is a passionately feminist spellbinder, a fluidly staged collection of vivid narrative pieces, some in prose and some in free verse, performed by seven young black women. It is almost exclusively concerned with the cavalier and sometimes downright brutal treatment accorded black women by their men. The play also captures the inner feelings of today's black women and goes beyond that to achieve its own kind of universality. Though their performances are mainly solo, the girls are united in much the same way as the cast in "A Chorus Line"—sometimes they sing together and on occasion dance together. And they are always united in sorrow, spirit, pride and soul. ". . . a triumphant event . . . filled with humor . . . joyous and alive, affirmative in the face of despair, and pure theatre."—N.Y. Daily News. ". . . a poignant, gripping, angry and beautiful theatre work."—Time. ". . . bitingly alive . . . overwhelming in its emotional impact . . . tragic, funny, proud and compassionate. . . ."—Newsweek.

(Royalty, $50-$40.)

EXCELLENT NEW

BLACK Plays

AND I AIN'T FINISHED YET (musical)—BETWEEN
NOW AND THEN—THE BRIXTON RECOVERY—
COLORED PEOPLE'S TIME—COMIN' UPTOWN
(musical)—DO LORD REMEMBER ME—DON'T
BOTHER ME, I CAN'T COPE (musical)—EDEN—
THE FIRST (musical)—FOR COLORED GIRLS WHO
HAVE CONSIDERED SUICIDE/WHEN THE RAINBOW
IS ENUF—FROM OKRA TO GREENS—HUNTER!—
IN THE MIDNIGHT HOUR—IT'S SO NICE TO BE
CIVILIZED (musical)—A LESSON FROM ALOES—
LIVIN' FAT—MASTER HAROLD . . . AND THE BOYS—
MEETINGS—OPEN ADMISSIONS (full-length & one-act
versions)—A PHOTOGRAPH: LOVERS IN MOTION—
A SOLIDER'S PLAY—SPELL #7—STEAL AWAY—
WELFARE—ZOOMAN AND THE SIGN

Consult our *Basic Catalogue of Plays* for details